to think
to dare
to dream

**OXLEY COLLEGE
BOWRAL 1983–2023**

40

**1983 TO 2023
OXLEY COLLEGE**

Amanda Mackevicius

Oxley College acknowledges the Gundungurra and Tharawal people as the
Traditional Custodians of the land we now call the Southern Highlands or Wingecarribee Shire.
We pay respect to Elders past and present and extend that respect
to all First Nations people.

Published by Oxley College
1-29 Railway Rd, Burradoo NSW 2576
61 2 4861 1366 / office@oxley.nsw.edu.au / www.oxley.nsw.edu.au

©Oxley College, 2023

ISBN 9780987624758
to think, to dare, to dream, Oxley College Bowral 1983–2023

Author: Amanda Mackevicius, amanda@mygenealogy.com.au
Page design Natalie Bowra, natalie@bowra.com.au
Cover design Lauren Babula
Printed in Australia by Ingram Spark

Contents

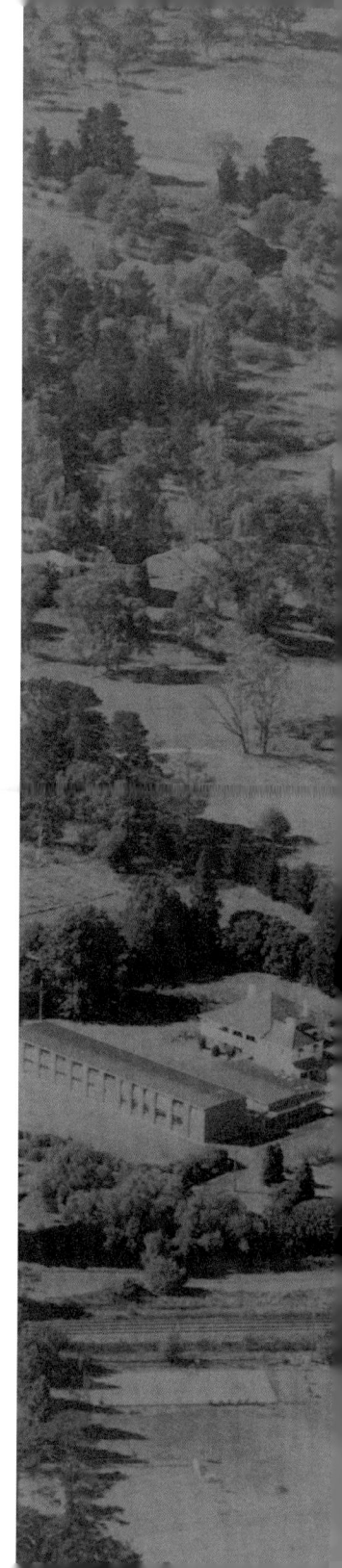

Forewords

The 40th birthday of a person is a time of celebration and reflection of the experiences of the first half of life, and of contemplation of the second half yet to come. For a school, a 40th birthday is also a time of celebration and reflection. This wonderful book by acclaimed biographer Amanda Mackevicius, documents in words and images the growth of Oxley College from a dream, to a thriving and well-established school. Over the past 40 years Oxley has faced challenges, such as the global financial crisis and COVID, and yet over its lifetime the school's overall trend has been one of consistent, remarkable progress. Oxley started as a dream to establish an independent, co-educational, non-denominational school for the families of the Southern Highlands and from a small school of less than thirty students, over two and a half thousand former Oxley students now roam the planet. We're now a school of 830, a size that is 'big enough to cater and small enough to care' as the former Head of College Chris Welsh used to say.

Throughout its 40 years, Oxley has become entwined in the lives of its many students, staff and the broader community. As a student in the late 1980s, I found Oxley to be a place of calm and kindness, of academic freedom of thought, and a strong, caring community. As a parent of three children who have attended Oxley College, these same attributes, distilled in the values of kindness, courage and wisdom have continued to enrich all of our lives. As a Governor and Chair of the Oxley College Board, it has been a great pleasure to see Oxley thrive. It is a joy to see former students, extended families and new families all benefit from the experience of Oxley as it has grown and developed, and yet at its core, remained the same, special place.

A 40th birthday for a school is also time for contemplation of the future. More like a Pin Oak than a person, I hope to see Oxley flourish and grow for many generations to come and have every confidence that it will do so.

Dr Stephen Barnett
Chairman of the Oxley College Board of Governors

It gives me a great deal of pleasure to acknowledge Oxley College's 40th birthday.

When I was asked to join the Board of Governors by former Chairman, the late Murray Walker, I had already experienced a minor role introducing a new banker to the College. I did not realise at the time that I would serve a period of just short of twelve exciting years as a Governor and later, as Chairman of the Board of Governors.

Over that time, I have seen the development of the Junior School and the commencement of the building master plan to provide Oxley College with the broad range of facilities students deserve. Each year, I have enjoyed participating in various assemblies, the annual Speech Night, orientation days, and viewed the excitement and emotion of the final year 12 assembly. Also, students displayed their talented skills and learning in major drama productions, musical evenings, and their contribution towards art in the higher school certificate. I listened with amazement of the achievements of past students when they returned to the College to address the Foundation Day ceremony.

I have had the rewarding experience of working with several wonderful Governors who always devoted their time willingly and brought to the table a wealth of practical knowledge.

It has not always been plain sailing. The global financial crisis affected enrolments quite seriously and only through the dedication of past Heads of College and staff, the College recovered. Over the intervening period of my time as Chairman and subsequently, I have been proud to see the improvement of overall academic results, as well as outstanding success in the arts and on the sporting fields.

Happy 40th birthday, Oxley College – I extend to you every good wish for your continued success.

Frank Conroy AM
Chairman of the Oxley College Board of Governors 2009–2020

Parents and Friends Association

As we celebrate the 40th birthday of Oxley College it is worth reflecting on the vision and courage of the parents who worked tirelessly to establish our school here in the Southern Highlands. Looking through the archives, the evidence of this bold and brave campaign is apparent in the advertisements placed to find students and the documentation of original meetings as they sought to build a new school. As members of the Oxley community, we are indebted to this group for their devotion, achievement and determination.

Given this parent-initiated campaign to establish the College, it is only fitting that an active and involved Parents and Friends Association (P&F) is the legacy of Oxley's founders. Over the 40 years of the College's existence, there have always been countless individuals and groups of people, volunteering and generously contributing their time, energy, ideas, and skills for the benefit of the students and the school community.

All parents of students at Oxley College automatically become members of the Oxley P&F when they join the school. A support body for the College both in a friend-raising and fundraising capacity, the P&F provides a great way for parents to get to know each other while raising funds for special projects and equipment around the school. In the past 20 years, funds raised have contributed to the Outback camping trailer, art kiln, K–6 playground equipment, interactive white boards, library infrastructure, the *Elvo* reception audio visual display, the vegetable garden project, sports scoreboard and a grand piano.

Over the years, the P&F has run a number of social activities and parent gatherings including the Pin Oak Fair, Eve on the Green event, text book exchange, Trivia Quiz evenings, twilight golf, a scavenger hunt through Burradoo, and a Thank You function at the end of each school year. Our parent community has also been involved in assisting at the annual Equestrian Day and previous Back to Oxley Days.

With the introduction of our Junior School, we have established a system of Parent year representatives, responsible for coordinating functions and providing a central point of contact with each year group. This network of parents organises several functions each year and is a vital link in the friend-raising experience at Oxley.

This year as we celebrate our 40th birthday we look forward to a year of bringing our College community back together. In the last few years our parent population has been affected by isolation regulations and limitations on social gatherings. For many new families, who have moved to the area for schooling, this has been a difficult time. In line with the College's 2023 theme of 'Regeneration', the P&F looks forward to restoring and reinforcing the important role that we play in developing relationships within our community.

Indeed, the P&F continues to be an unbroken thread that weaves throughout the 'lovingly woven tapestry' of Oxley College.

Megan Moore
Parents and Friends Association, President 2020–2023

Opposite: Members of the 2023 Parents and Friends Committee.
Left to right: Samantha Spring, Lauren Bloom, Sooz Heinrich, Megan Moore, Rebecca Morse and Sally Kean.

Introduction

To celebrate the 21st birthday of Oxley College in 2004, a book titled *A Lovingly Woven Tapestry, Oxley College Bowral 1983–2004* was published. Commissioned by the then Board of Governors and written by esteemed author and historian Linda Emery, a former Oxley Governor and parent, *A Lovingly Woven Tapestry* comprehensively documents the history, challenges and successes of the early years of the College and captures the essence of what it means to be part of the Oxley family. For your digital copy of *A Lovingly Woven Tapestry Tapestry, Oxley College Bowral 1983–2004* visit the Oxley College website About Page www.oxley.nsw.edu.au/about/the-college or scan the QR code on the last page of this book.

In recognition of Oxley's 40th birthday and to acknowledge the achievements, major changes and significant milestones in the life of Oxley College since 2005, *To Think, To Dare, To Dream – Oxley College Bowral 1983–2023* picks up the threads of Oxley's evolving history. Reflecting on the past 40 years of the life of the College, the book aims to celebrate and encapsulate some of what it is that makes Oxley College so special.

Just as the history of Oxley College has shaped its present, the school's future will be determined by who we are now and what we do next.

Legacy, a retrospective

What does it mean to leave a legacy? Alexander Reichenfeld, a Year 12 student in 2021, explored this question in relation to the land Oxley occupies. His insights, published in *Pin Oak* edition 131, follow:

... I thought of the traditional custodians of this land, the Gundungurra people, whose country includes Burradoo – 'a place of many brigalow trees' – and the land upon which we have been privileged to receive our education.

In acknowledging this as Aboriginal and Torres Strait Islander land, I cast my mind back to a 'Big History' lesson in Year 10, where my then teacher, Mr Braddock, tried to help us perceive the age of the universe by imagining it as a timeline the width of the classroom. On that scale, we understand the human timeline to be a paper-thin sliver in the vast expanse of time the universe has existed. Similarly, to grasp the perpetuity of continuous cultural connection between our First Nations peoples and this entire continent, I'll try converting something massive into a more manageable scale for the purposes of clarity.

So here we go. Oxley College will celebrate its 40th anniversary in 2023. That's two generations. Australia has recognised itself as a nation for around six generations. The historical figure of Jesus Christ, whose teachings have shaped the ethics and morality of millions of Australians, walked the earth about 100 generations ago. The First Nations people of Australia have been traditional custodians of this continent for over 3,000 continuous generations, as I understand it, a minimum 60,000 year history of unbroken relationship with country. And Aboriginal nations did so with such skill, knowledge and understanding on the driest inhabited continent on the planet that their harmonious relationship with nature now offers a guide to a more sustainable future. This is a legacy for humanity.

On a generational scale then, Oxley College itself represents the paper-thin, knife-edge sliver of time. Put another way, if Oxley College were included in a 3,000 page book, Australian History, we would appear on the last page. Federation would be five pages earlier. As the oldest living culture on Earth, the First Nations people of Australia are considered the first amongst First Nations people globally. It is only right that we pay our respects to Elders, past and present.

On behalf of the class of 2021, I am honoured to have shared my learning experiences on the ancestral lands of the traditional custodians, the Gundungurra people and I pay respect to Elders past and present. I recognise that First Australians never ceded sovereignty. This continent always was and always will be Aboriginal and Torres Strait Islander land.

Alexander Reichenfeld, Year 12, 2021

Before Oxley

Long before the first Europeans passed through the Southern Highlands in 1798, the land on which Oxley College stands was a part of the traditional lands of the Gundungurra people. The Wingecarribee River was the focus of their day-to-day lives, where they camped, fished for eels and hunted kangaroos from the enormous mobs that once ranged the open grasslands along the riverbank. White settlement of the area began in 1819 when Doctor Charles Throsby, led by Aboriginal guides, set up camp on the river at Bong Bong.

Linda Emery
A Lovingly Woven Tapestry, Oxley College Bowral 1983–2004

1837

100 acre land grant is made to former convict, William Hutchinson, who arrived in New South Wales in 1799. Oxley College occupies land inherited by William's grandson, Mackenzie Bowman Hutchinson. The complete history of the property known as *Elvo* can be found in Chapter 1 of *A Lovingly Woven Tapestry, Oxley College Bowral 1983–2004* which can be accessed via the QR code on the last page of this book.

Photo: Tim Mooney, 1985

1867

The Great Southern Railway reached Picton in 1863 and went on to Moss Vale via Bowral in 1867. With the opening of the railway the townships of Mittagong, Bowral and Moss Vale began to grow.

1881

The 1880s were boom years in the district. The Oxley College site was subdivided into 'Villa Sites' and purchased by William Vero Read, of Sydney, who sold it to Septimus Alfred Stephen in 1882.

c1884

Elvo, an anagram of the word 'love', was built by Septimus Alfred Stephen as his family's summer holiday home. The seventh son of Sir Alfred Stephen, Chief Justice of New South Wales from 1844 to 1873, Septimus was one of the three founding partners of the Sydney Law Firm Stephen, Jacques and Stephen. One of his older brothers, Montagu Consett Stephen, was the other partner named Stephen. Septimus's son, Colin, and grand-son, Alistair, also served as senior partners of the firm, known today as King & Wood Mallesons.

Septimus Stephen married Lucy Campbell, the daughter of Robert Campbell of Duntroon. He later moved to England, as did all of his children, apart from his third child, Colin Campbell Stephen (born 1872). In 2013 some of Colin's descendants established the Stephen Bursary, to perpetuate the link between the Stephen family and Oxley College. Now known as the Stephen Family Award, it is presented annually to the Year 11 Dux.

1911

Elvo, on 45 acres, sold to Arthur Wigram Allen, of the legal firm formerly known as Allen, Allen and Hemsley. The house was largely used as a summer retreat. Arthur's daughter, Margaret Allen (later Lady Gifford), planted the acorn which grew into Oxley's much loved Pin Oak tree, which graces the *Elvo* lawn.

1912

Allen family members and friends on the verandah of *Elvo*, the country house of Arthur Wigram, Burradoo, February 1912.

1914

Mary Sloman in the garden of *Elvo*, the Allen family country house, Burradoo, March 1914.

Images courtesy Berrima District Historical Society

1920

Elvo sold to Sir John Garvan and his five siblings, Gerald, Anne, Clare, Nina and Helena, who each held a one sixth share in the property. Their father, James Patrick Garvan, pioneered the insurance industry in Australia, forming the City Mutual Life and Fire Insurance companies. Under Sir John Garvan the companies amalgamated to become the Mutual Life and Citizens Assurance Company, or MLC. Sir John Garvan, a generous philanthropist and sportsman, became a Director, and later Chairman of the Commonwealth Bank, and was knighted before his death in 1927. His sister, Helena, married Professor Arthur Mills and purchased all the shares in *Elvo*. The Garvan Institute of Medical Research at St Vincent's Hospital is named in memory of James Patrick Garvan and his family, through a gift of £100,000 from Helena Mills in 1960.

You Will Enjoy a Country
Holiday at

"ELVO" BURRADOO

Unexcelled Cuisine, Comfort and
Convenience for 15 Guests.

☆

TARIFF £11/11/- to £13/13/-

☆

Mrs. WILLIAMS
BOWRAL 47

M _____

_____

_____

_____

1953

Elvo, by now on 57 acres after the purchase of additional land, is sold at auction to George Williams, who ran Hereford cattle and a few sheep on the land. His wife, Jean, converted *Elvo* into a guest house, offering 'unexcelled cuisine, comfort and convenience' to about fifteen guests, many of whom had children boarding at local schools: Tudor House, Frensham and SCEGGS.

1959

Elvo is purchased by a Catholic teaching order, De La Salle Brothers, for use as a Juniorate for boys in their final secondary years who wished to enter the priesthood. It was the Juniorate from 1959 to 1966 and the Novitiate from 1967 to 1977.

Elvo 1953, during George Williams' ownership

1962

The Brothers converted the *Elvo* stables into classrooms, added a toilet block, an earthquake-proof classroom block, a catering building, oval and tennis courts. The new De La Salle classroom block opened in April 1964.

1965

The De La Salle Brothers operated the Bowral Weather Station from *Elvo*, on behalf of the Commonwealth Bureau of Meteorology, from December 1965 until 1982. It was then taken over by Mr and Mrs Jarratt, who lived nearby. A report in the first edition of *The Oxleyan* magazine (Vol 1, 1983, p.91) states:

Bowral weather, apparently, is important in determining weather patterns and problems for aircraft flying between Sydney and Melbourne. The techniques of recording the weather have changed little over the years, with a Stevenson Screen and Wind Vane obvious to any casual observer. Recordings are made every three hours, except for midnight, and include cloud cover and height, wind speed and direction, visibility, maximum and minimum temperature, dry and wet temperatures, and rainfall.

At first, the De La Salle Brothers sent their information to the Sydney Weather Bureau by telegram consisting of coded numbers. Over the weekends, when there was no one at the Bowral Telegram office, a trunk line to the Sydney Telegram service was used. Later a telex machine (the first to be given to a district weather station in Australia) was installed and the Brothers sent their information to Melbourne, where it was placed on a computer and then sent simultaneously to Sydney and London (Greenwich is the world headquarters for weather data).

Recently a computer was added to the equipment and placed in the school cottage where the telex has also been placed. The present weather lady is Mrs Sally Jarrett, who is assisted by her husband when he is not overseas. Having the weather station on the property is a tremendous asset to the geography and science students.

1973

The possibility of starting a secondary school for boys in the area was floated by a group of parents who had sons attending Tudor House, Moss Vale.

1977

A revision of church policy saw the Novitiate relocate to Sydney when the last group of young men completed their training. The retired or semi-retired Brothers who remained at *Elvo*, cared for the grounds and made the property available for camps, seminars and retreats.

1978

A small group of parents attend a meeting at the junior Winifred West school, Gib Gate, called by Headmaster Dennis Chugg, to discuss the future secondary education of their sons.

1979

A public meeting was held in Bowral on 18 October to discuss a 'Proposed Independent Secondary School' and to ascertain the level of support. Over 100 people attended the meeting and voted to make the school co-educational.

Proposed Independent Secondary School

BOWRAL

PUBLIC MEETING
Thursday 18th October, 1979,
MEMORIAL HALL, BOWRAL.

INDEPENDENT BOYS SECONDARY SCHOOL PROPOSED FOR THE AREA

A group of parents who have boys approaching secondary school age have dedicated themselves to forming an independent secondary school for boys in the Bowral area. If the support they have had to date is any indication, then many other parents in the area also feel there is a need for a new private day school here.

"The depressing unemployment figures have rekindled the interest of most parents in the direction of their sons education", said Mr Grahame Smee, member of the steering committee, "they realise", he continued, "that the best education to develop meaningful long term employment goals in a child is a total education and not only mastering of the formal disciplines - language, science and mathematics".

The steering committee propose an orthodox system for the school coupled with many extra curricular activities, including cadets.

The committee hopes to develop "a school in which boys will achieve a balanced understanding and a joy in achieving success in the everyday needs of the head of a modern family" said committee member Mr Rick Tendys "and that includes learning how to strip and assemble his lawn mower, to how to build a solar powered contrivance and from first aid to growing his own vegetables".

"It will be a school which will teach boys respect for their government and respect for the traditions." said Mr Leo Berkelouw.

The committee is currently actively involved in investigating potential sites and buildings, collecting names of competent experienced and enthusiastic teaching staff for the school which is to have a maximum of 250 boys.

"The finance required to start the school is of course a major problem," said Mr Smee, "however, while we - the committee - hope that a benefactor genuinely interested in education may come forward with a large donation, members are nonetheless preparing to float a company and sell shares in the venture" he continued.

As the committee points out "to send a boy to boarding school in Sydney or Canberra the total cost to the Higher School Certificate level would cost approximately $50,000 plus of course, costs incurred in visiting the boy during the year and fares for him back to the family in holidays.

Obvious other disadvantages with sending boys away from the family are that parents do not want to lose contact with their children in those critical years from 11 to 17 and on the spot parents can liase closely with teachers.

The committee assumes that an initial investment of $300,000 would cut the education costs by 75% (75% of 50,000 - $37,000 per boy).

If the figure of $300,000 is divided by approximately 100 parents it would involve an investment of only $3,000 (...).

"A smallish school of 250-300 students offers a sufficient range of abilities to allow competition, yet the aims of the school will encourage self development and self reliance in harmonious accord with the traditional christian morals," said Mr Smee.

Classes will be small, all teachers will know all students and parents will with special qualifications will be welcomed to help in instructing their own specialties

"The boys will have opportunities to work in different positions during their holidays to give them an opportunity to select a career knowingly". said Mr Smee.

"This type of schooling both overseas and in Australia have been very successful" said Mr Smee "for example Braemar College and Eltham College in Victoria".

The committee will call a general meeting of interested parents in October (date yet to be set) to assess enrolments and to present the aims of the school in more detail.

"The present and long term aim is to establish a school which will immediately provide a high standard equivalent to long established private schools in Sydney and Canberra, it will be recognised by all existing private schools as well as tertiary and educational establishments" said Mr Smee.

If you would like further information on this proposed new independent boys secondary school which is planned to commence operation in 1981 phone Graham Smee or Rick Tendys.

● Members of the steering committee for the proposed independent secondary boys school are seated from left to right Alec Mell, Rob Limebeer, Rick Tendys and Owain Rowland-Jones. Standing are Leo Berkelouw (left) and Grahame Smee.

Southern Highlands News October 1979

1980

Ongoing discussions about founding an independent, co-educational, non-denominational day school in the Southern Highlands. On 9 November an Open Day, entitled 'Under the Marquee', was the first official fund raising function held on the school campus, which was still operating as De La Salle College.

1981

The interim Board of Governors continued planning throughout 1981, meeting at *Ambleside*, the Mittagong home of Don and Betty Hoskins.

The De La Salle property c 1981 with cattle grazing on what is now Founders Field

Oxley was founded in quite a hostile environment. Many believed resources could have been better spent elsewhere. Many, believing independent education divided society, were in principle implacably opposed to the College's establishment. Sceptics imagined the school would quickly founder as other similar establishments in the district had done.

Among the reasons, then, for instituting a Foundation Day celebration was a feeling that we needed regularly to refine the vision; to bring before ourselves and the community at large what it was for which Oxley stood: what was important about it; why it needed preserving and nurturing.

Extract from Dr David Wright's Foundation Day speech, 2008

John Joseph William
Molesworth Oxley,
1810, miniature
watercolour portrait.

Courtesy State Library of
New South Wales

Oxley College was named after John Joseph William Molesworth Oxley (1785–1828) a Naval officer, explorer, philanthropist, politician, businessman and surveyor general to the Colony of New South Wales. John Oxley's descendants kindly allowed their family crest and motto, *Patientia et Fortitudine* – Patience and Fortitude, to be adopted as the College badge and motto.

The Oxley name has been associated with the Southern Highlands from the earliest days of white exploration and settlement in the area. In 1816 John Oxley sent stock from his Camden property to graze in the area known as Wingecarribee, land that would be granted to him in June 1823. This property of 2,300 acres he named Westow, which took in much of the land between present day Berrima and Bowral.

Nearly 30 years after Oxley's death, and in recognition of his services to the colony in exploration and surveying, the British government approved two grants totalling 5,000 acres to his sons. John Norton Oxley and Henry Molesworth Oxley were just two and four years old when their father died and left the family in precarious financial circumstances.

Anticipating the growth that would follow the opening of the rail link with Sydney, solicitor John Norton Oxley subdivided some of this land in 1863 as the Private Township of Bowral. His brother, Henry Molesworth Oxley, was responsible for the building in 1857 of Wingecarribee, a prefabricated iron 'kit-house' imported from England, which still nestles elegantly on the slopes of Oxley Hill*. Three generations of the Oxley family lived in the house until it passed to a nephew of Mrs Vera Oxley, friend and benefactor of Oxley College.

Linda Emery, *A Lovingly Woven Tapestry* (The Oxley Family)

---

*The College enjoys rural views across to Oxley Hill

Oxley becomes
a reality

1982

Oxley College Limited was incorporated as a public company on 12 January 1982. The first meeting of the Foundation Governors of the Board of Oxley College Limited took place at *Ambleside* on 8 February 1982. Members of the Board and first members of the company were Donald Hoskins, Leo Berkelouw, Peter Bray (Public Officer/Treasurer), Bill Carpenter (Secretary), Margaret Chambers, Stephen Harrison, Ian McKenzie, Graham Smee and Rick Tendys. Don Hoskins was elected Founding Chairman, a position he held until March 1988.

On 18 June 1982, the Prime Minister, Malcolm Fraser, and Member for Macarthur, Michael Baume, jointly announced a conditional financial grant from the Commonwealth Schools Commission towards the purchase of 5.59 hectares of land from the Trustees of the De La Salle Brothers and the renovation of existing buildings for use as a school.

David Hugh Morley Wright was offered the position of Headmaster of Oxley College on 6 July 1982. Born in Salisbury, Rhodesia, David was a Rhodes Scholar and graduate of three universities. He moved to Australia from Rhodesia in 1981 with his wife Kelly and their two daughters, to begin a new chapter in their lives. More information about David's life can be found in *A Lovingly Woven Tapestry*, p.38.

A 'million dollar' school... set up by parents

In a country town, three families sought to find the best in education

A dentist's chair played a persuasive role filling gaps in a new school's Board of Governors. "An offer I couldn't refuse," remembers the chairman, retired engineer Don Hoskins who was in the hot seat.

So was Bill Carpenter, a valuer, who agreed to be secretary through a mouthful of instruments: "I had no choice," he said later.

The hands that held those coercive instruments at Bowral, the NSW Southern Highlands township, were those of dentist Grahame Smee.

While a battle about the funding of private schools in Australia raged, Grahame, two friends and their wives decided to take a hand in the education of their children by founding a co-ed day college.

Now, the land and buildings bought, a principal appointed, crest created and "traditional, conservative" uniforms being made, places are being filled for 1983 when, beginning with years seven and eight, their dream of Oxley College becomes reality.

"It's been a hard slog," says Grahame. "Some of our early supporters said, when they looked at the problems, that it couldn't be done. They dropped out. We found others who wouldn't take no for an answer and we did it."

Another of the founders, Ric Tendys, a Qantas flight service director and former school teacher, says the district was crowded with couples who had moved from the city to find a better way of life for their children.

But they were disappointed with existing public and private schools.

"We didn't want our children to go away to boarding school for their high school years," says Ric. "But the existing schools all seemed to be bulging at the seams and fighting for smaller classes and community support."

"Imagine the situation: three families with very little spare cash and not really up-to-date with modern schooling, embark on a $1 million project to ensure their children have the best education possible in high school. Impossible?"

They began by looking at sites and found what they wanted in a former De la Salle novitiate at nearby Burradoo. It included the handsome homestead on the Elvo Estate, facing the land granted to early explorer and Surveyor-General, John Oxley.

The newly-formed Board of Governors applied for — and was granted — a $600,000 building grant from the Commonwealth Schools Commission. Vendor finance and other locally-raised funds made the $1 million college possible.

Next job was to appoint a principal. From dozens of applicants, a Rhodesian-born Rhodes Scholar, David Wright, was selected. He had been involved in starting schools overseas.

The task of building a tradition at a new school in the country doesn't daunt him at all.

"We have one great advantage," he says. "Oxley College is a product of a community's concern for its children.

"Parents are fearful of the sort of ideology, the permissive, unionist line that seems to be making itself felt in the NSW Teachers' Federation," he said.

"Instead of teachers helping children, they're looking after their own interests. That won't be so at Oxley."

Within a few years, it's hoped about 350 boys and girls will be receiving a "disciplined" education in things "aesthetic and creative, ethical, linguistic, mathematical, physical, scientific, social and political, and spiritual."

One of the non-profit college's aims, says the chairman Don Hoskins, will be to keep career options open to students for as long as possible in a fast-changing world.

An unusual attraction for students will be the meteorological station in the school grounds. The playing fields of Burradoo include five tennis courts, a basketball court and two large ovals.

"We have the best turf cricket pitch in the district," says Ric Tendys. "That's as it should be — this is Don Bradman country."

— KEN BRASS

Principal David Wright with parents and prospective pupils. Picture: Neville Waller.

THE AUSTRALIAN WOMEN'S WEEKLY — OCTOBER 20, 1982

31

Australian Women's Weekly 20 October 1982 (p.31)

1983

Oxley College opened on 2 February 1983 with an initial enrolment of 24 students in Years 7 and 8 and four full-time teachers. The Parents and Friends Association was formed in February 1983 and the official opening of the school, by Mrs Vera Oxley, took place on 4 November 1983.

> As individual as that tree is (the splendid oak on the front lawn) as proud as that tree is to stand on its own, it is only so individual, so proud, as long as it remains rooted in the soil which has nourished it.
>
> *Helmut Schaefer, first Year 12 Form Master*

Oxley College

CO-EDUCATIONAL   INDEPENDENT   SECONDARY

COLLEGE OPEN DAY

• Standing impressively at the entrance, the new Oxley College sign indicates that the college is now open for business. Across the cricket oval one can see the school buildings which presently reverberate to the sound of workmen's tools. Very good progress is being made with the major renovations which are being undertaken. The College is having an Open Day commencing at 11am on Sunday, November 16. Everyone who is interested would be very welcome to attend then, to see the development that has taken place and to hear about plans for the future. Barbecue facilities will be available and meat, rolls, salad and drinks will be on sale. Those who would prefer to bring their own picnic lunches would be very welcome. Pictured under the sign is Oxley College Headmaster, Mr. David Wright, B.Sc Agric., M.A., M.Ed., U.E.D.

Headmaster David Wright and the original school entry board. A school 'Open Day' was held on Sunday 16 November 1982.

Eternally end begets beginning and the foundation students will not have suffered from their experience in risking, in providing answers, in moulding and forging a new school.

Foundation staff member Peter Craig, in the editorial of the first edition of The Oxleyan *magazine. Mr Craig initially taught English, Maths, History, Phys Ed and Sport and was* The Oxleyan *editor for many years. He was appointed Deputy Headmaster in March 1985.*

Foundation staff and students, 2 February 1983 (left to right) Back row: Mr L Mann, Mrs G Graves, Mr D Stanford, Miss M Bennett, Mr D Wright, (Headmaster), Mrs C Zakaria, Mrs C Wright, Mrs M Laguna, Mr P Craig and Mrs V Craig. Middle row: C Warby, A Fennell, N McDonald, G Lampert, J Law, D Olliver, A Colless, M Lowe, R Stuart, J Parker, C Bull, M Close, T Watson. Front row: J Clinton, M Mitchell, T Davidson, A Maher, T Hayes, M Wainberg, S Crittle, T Butterfield, S Gill, C McKenzie, K Close.

● Librarian at the new Oxley College in Bowral is Mrs Kelly Wright, wife of the Headmaster, seen here in the well-equipped Library with Mrs Betty Hoskins, wife of the Chairman of the Board of Governors, and Mrs Margaret Chambers, who is one of the Governors.

The published caption reads: Librarian at the new Oxley College in Bowral is Mrs Kelly Wright, wife of the Headmaster, seen here in the well-equipped Library with Mrs Betty Hoskins, wife of the Chairman of the Board of Governors, and Mrs Margaret Chambers, who is one of the Governors.

1983 Athletics team (left to right) T Watson, D Olliver, V John, J Law, M Close, G Lambert, T Hayes, K Close, M Mitchell, J Parker, A Maher, C Warby, N Murray-Leslie, M Lowe, R Veldhuis, B Smedley, Mr P Craig (coach).

THE

OXLEYAN

Vol. 1 1983

First edition of *The Oxleyan*

1984

75 students, six full-time teachers. Additional two acres of land was purchased and a second sports oval was built (combined cost $80,000). Construction of staff study rooms, the Music Centre, student lockers and three tennis courts (approximate cost $18,000).

Peter and Betty Bray generously offered to gift ten acres of land on the opposite side of the Wingecarribee River (Bray Fields) for future sports field development.

Oxley students participated in the Duke of Edinburgh Award for the first time.

Catching practice before a cricket game

1985

138 students, eight full-time and four part-time staff members.

Construction of Art Room, two classrooms, two Science laboratories, boys' toilet, library and staff room.

Early school camp. Parent Bob Mitchell transported camping gear to Bungonia in his truck.

OXLEY COLLEGE

1985 Master Plan brochure

1986

221 students at the school, with three Year 7 streams for the first time.

Four new classrooms were built along with girls' toilets, staff study areas and a connecting walkway.

OXLEY COLLEGE AND THE SCHOOLS' DEVELOPMENT

An independent, co-educational, non-denominational, secondary day school functioning as a non-profit organisation under the control of a Board of Governors.

A school of the community established by the community to endeavour to serve that community by providing a particular style of education, which seeks:

1. To foster the highest standard in academic, sporting and cultural pursuits.

2. To create that environment of discipline and respect for the great historical and Christian traditions as might best develop genuine freedom and a mature understanding of truth, goodness and virtue.

3. To stress the worth of individual persons and a proper regard for good manners, courteous behaviour and neatness of dress and deportment.

4. To promote those activities most likely to produce full, balanced, creative human beings with a developed sense of citizenship.

The College, in its third year of operation, now needs to complete the originally planned facilities, and in the face of considerable demand for places, must now expand. An on-going appeal is now being made to parents and friends to help the College continue with its educational service to the community.

Contributions to the Oxley College School Building Fund are under present legislation fully tax-deductible.

The Governors: D. G. Hoskins M.I.E. Aust. (Chairman), Dr C. M. Smee B.D.S. Syd. (Vice-Chairman), W. McL. Carpenter (Secretary), P. M. Bray A.C.A. (Treasurer), D. H. Bareby, L. L. Berkelouw, Mrs. M. Chambury, S. B. M. Harrison M.Ed. (Bursar Syd. Uni.), Dr I. C. McKinnon M.B. Ch.B. (Edin.), F.R.A.C.A.S., R. Tendys.

Headmaster: Mr. David H. M. Wright B.Sc. Agric. (Natal), M.A. (Oxon.), M.Ed. (U.B.), U.E.D.

FIRST PHASE

1982   Purchase of former De La Salle Novitiate. Initial stage of refurbishing of facilities and procuring of equipment to meet Commonwealth and State requirements. Cost — $1,000,000 Commonwealth Schools Commission Contribution $606,000.

1983   College opened with 24 foundation students and 4 full-time teachers.

1984   Enrolment 79, 6 full-time teachers.
Purchase of 2 acres of land and establishment of new sporting oval $80,000.
Construction of main steps, staff study rooms, music centre, pupil lockers, 3 new tennis courts. Approximately $18,000.
In spite of small enrolment, a small operating profit recorded for the year.

1985   Enrolment 138, 8 full-time, 4 part-time members of teaching staff.
Decision taken to enrol 3 streams in Year 7 in 1986.
Total donations to Building Fund in First Phase — $65,000.

THE SCHOOL 1983-1990

| | ACTUAL | | | | PROJECTED | | |
	1983	1984	1985	1986	1987	1988	1989	1990
Year 7	14	38	51	75	75	75	75	75
Year 8	10	19	40	50	75	75	75	75
Year 9	—	19	26	40	50	75	75	75
Year 10			21	26	40	50	75	75
Year 11	—	—	—	25	30	40	50	60
Year 12	—	—	—	—	25	30	40	50
TOTAL	24	76	138	216	295	345	390	410

Page from 1985 School's Development brochure

1987

280 students. The administrative area was remodeled and an adjoining acre of land was purchased to extend the recreational grounds. The first group of students completed their Higher School Certificate, the Old Oxleyans Association was formed and the College gardens were awarded first prize in the school section of the Bowral Tulip Time Competition. Parent volunteers, co-ordinated by Kelly Wright (Oxley's Librarian and the Headmaster's wife) had revitalised the overgrown and neglected gardens. In *A Lovingly Woven Tapestry*, p.54, Kelly reflected:

The parents were incredibly committed in every way, so they would respond to my call for a working bee. Arriving with picks and shovels and the dreaded chain saws. We chopped back years of old growth, planted trees, moved whole beds and enjoyed many tired barbecues on the front lawn. One of our most exciting occasions was when we discovered the pottery edging and then the pathway running around the side garden (later called the Headmaster's Wife's Garden). It had lain buried beneath years of soil, and leaf build up.

First Year 12 Tree Planting, Foundation Day 1987. The simple ritual of planting of a tree in the College grounds on Foundation Day, by the Head Boy and Head Girl with assistance from the youngest students at the College, is an annual tradition. As symbols of growth and renewal, the trees provide a physical reminder of past Year 12 students and for those who are leaving, a sense that something of themselves remains at Oxley.

Two roads diverged in a wood, and I —
I took the one less travelled by,
And that has made all the difference.

Extract from fourth stanza of 'The Road Not Taken' by American poet Robert Frost (1874–1963). This framed quotation, a favourite of David Wright, hung in the library named after him, for many years. In A Lovingly Woven Tapestry, Linda Emery wrote, 'The Founding Headmaster, himself a poet, was fond of quoting it in the context of Oxley College and its students daring to be different – 'risking the unknown terrain' and the words had great resonance for the pioneers of the 1980s'.

The cover of an eight page booklet produced in 1988 containing facts and trivia about Oxley College.

Oxley College

Did you know?

"The old Elvo garden gave us the skeleton of Oak and Horse Chestnut, Elm and Deodar, Holly and Liquidambar all underplanted with Spring Daffodils, Bluebells, Ranunculas, Freesias, Hyacinths, Snowdrops, Crocus and Iris. A clay tiled pathway was revealed under the weeds along with Forget-me-Nots, Lavender, Rosemary, Alyssum, Ajuga, Violets, Agapanthus and a Laurel hedge.
The new garden plantings are for children – for nooks and crannies, for relaxation, calm and beauty." – Kelly Wright

Oxley College

Railway Parade, Burradoo. P.O. Box 552, Bowral, N.S.W. 2576
Telephone: (048) 611 366

1988

315 students. 29 teachers provided 31 Year 12 students with a choice of 20 subjects. Construction of the Home Science classroom, Music rooms and a staff study.

Inaugural Outback trip to Central Australia. Devised by teacher Helmut Schaefer, the annual trip is a rite of passage for Year 11 students.

By 1988 the Parents and Friends Association was contributing more than $20,000 a year to various projects at the College. This year they purchased six kayaks for the Canoe Club.

Home Science students

Canoe Club 1988. Kayaking, as it was better known, was introduced to encourage the development of a wide range of skills including advanced boat handling techniques for white water and slalom. A supervised boatbuilding program enabled students to build a fibreglass kayak, in their own time.

Timeless Oxley Outback scene

1989

342 students. Renovation and extension of Hoskins Hall. To honour the contribution to Oxley College of the Founding Chairman, Don Hoskins, the building was named Hoskins Hall.

1990

353 students. 17th and 18th classrooms constructed. Volume 1, Number 1 of *The Old Ox*, was published by an editorial committee of Old Oxleyans.

A single story Hoskins Hall pre-renovations

On Speech Day, 1989, the Oxley College Clothing Pool presented the school with a lectern made of Australian Cedar (Toona Australis) with Queensland White Beech (Gemlina) in the crest. The lectern was crafted by Bernadette Foley at Sturt Mittagong and is still in use.

Oxley College

SCHOOL BUILDING FUND

APPEAL

JANUARY 1989

The great success and rapid growth of Oxley College require us to proceed immediately with building the next stage of the School's Master Plan.

THIS APPEAL IS TO RAISE THE FUNDS REQUIRED FOR THIS IMPORTANT DEVELOPMENT OF THE COLLEGE.

THE AIMS OF THIS STAGE OF DEVELOPMENT ARE:

"To accommodate the whole school in assembly; to further promote the excellent standards already achieved in drama, music, public speaking and debating; to provide a multi-purpose hall and gymnasium; satisfactorily to accommodate a highly qualified and dedicated staff".

(D. H. M. Wright ~Headmaster)

1989 Building Appeal brochure

"The dream we had was to have a distinctive school, because schools do make a difference. Oxley is unique because it is the product of a community determined to do something to provide what it believes is important in education. Enormous risks were taken. Great faith was exhibited. The community rallied to support. The progress has been remarkable."

(D H M Wright – Headmaster)

A VISION UNFOLDS

1991

375 students. Formulation of Strategic Plan for the years 1991 to 2000.

The inaugural meeting of The Old Oxleyans Association was held in July 1991, after the annual winter sports (games) against the school. Chaired by the Secretary of the Board of Governors, Bill Carpenter, the first committee of ex-students was elected, with Trish Varvel (1988) as President.

Linda Emery, *A Lovingly Woven Tapestry*, p.134

1992

In September Oxley celebrated the 10th anniversary of the founding of the College. The 10th birthday of the actual opening of the school was celebrated in 1993. A publication titled *On Exultant Wings: Oxley Poems*, by David Wright, was published by the Parents and Friends Association.

10 Year Anniversary
Masked Ball
Foundation Weekend
Saturday 5th September

7.30 p.m. till late

Berrima Room
Resort Hotel Bowral Heritage Park

The Event of the Decade

Dining and Dancing
to the soothing sounds of
Back to Back

Black Tie / Lounge Suit

1993

Headmaster David Wright resigned at the end of the school year to take up a position as Principal of the Independent Grammar School in Sydney.

10th birthday celebrations and birthday cake

1994

Tony Nutt was Headmaster of Oxley College for six months.
Peter Craig was the acting Headmaster after his departure.

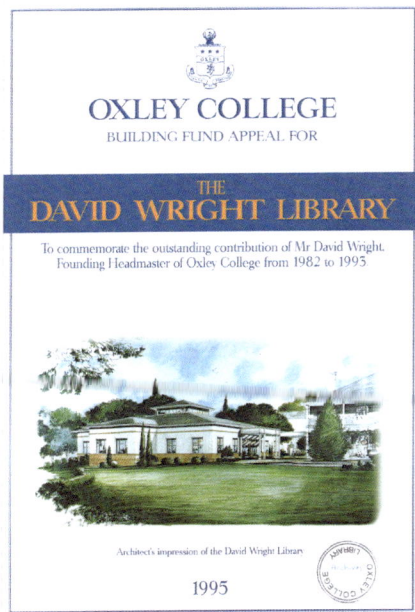

David Wright Library Building Fund Appeal
brochure

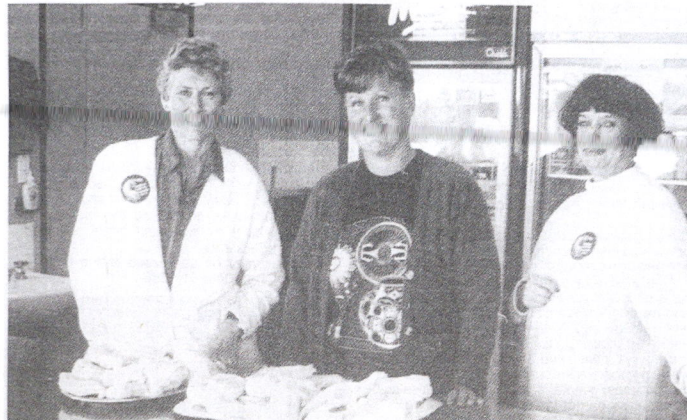

• Ready for the lunchtime rush at Oxley College's new canteen are (l to r) Janet
Hackleton from Kangaroo Valley, Denise Graham, canteen co-ordinator from
Robertson, and Anne McMillan from Mittagong. Over 40 women work on a rostered
basis to operate the college canteen.

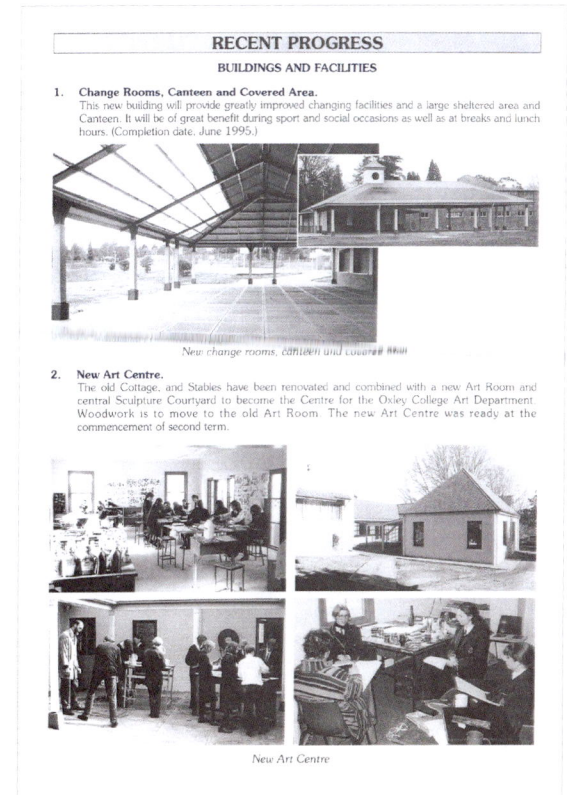

1995 *Oxley College Update* brochure, 'Recent Progress'

1995

Christopher Welsh commenced as Headmaster in July. On Foundation Day
a time capsule was placed in the wall of the David Wright Library, which
was being built at this time. The new Art Centre, canteen, change rooms
and covered outdoor area with clock tower and flagpole were opened.
This area, since remodeled, is now called The Pavilion.

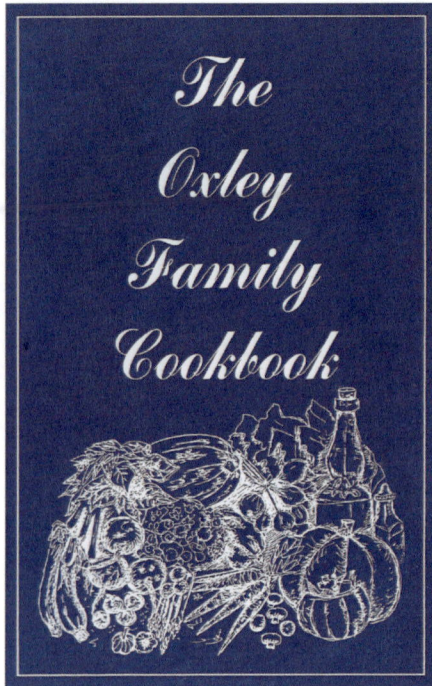

The Oxley Family Cookbook, published in 1995. Produced in association with the 1996 Oxley College Country Fair, *The Oxley Family Cookbook* contains 60 pages of recipes contributed by parents, students, teachers and friends of Oxley College. Edited by Susie and Catherine Dorsen with artwork by the 1995 Visual Arts Scholarship student Jennifer Hill (Years 11/12).

1996

Bi-annual Country Fair held at Oxley on 24 February and the David Wright Library opened on Foundation Day (7 September). The complete story of the changes and events taking place at Oxley during this time period can be read in 'Building the School', Chapter 7 of *A Lovingly Woven Tapestry*, p.109.

1997

Students have been involved with tree planting and river restoration for decades, since joining Sydney Water's river-monitoring program 'Streamwatch' in 1992.

Students planting trees on the banks of the Wingecarribee River, next to Bray Fields in June 1997

1998

450 students enrolled. Country Fair held at Oxley in March. Refurbished Science facilities opened.

1999

Art and Craft Fair held over June long weekend. Building Appeal launched to raise funds for new netball and tennis courts, Science laboratory, gymnasium and parking areas.

2000

Naming of Bray Fields and the Parents and Friends Tennis Courts, fourth Science laboratory built, Oxley Fair held 25 March.

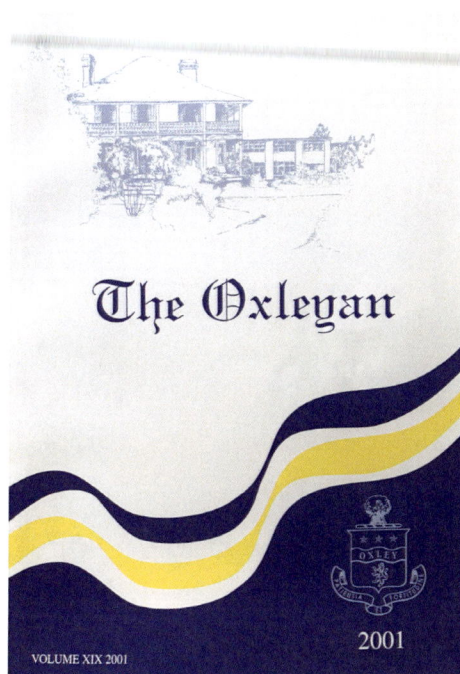

The Oxleyan, 2001

We must continue to water and to nurture
what others have planted before us
and as they grow stronger and bigger,
as we climb through their branches
towards the heavens,
as we shelter in their shade in times
of quiet reflection or from the heat of the day,
let us remember to plant and keep planting
what is worthwhile and strong
and secure for those in Kindergarten now
and for those who are yet to come.
And let us too remember those who planted for us, and be thankful.

Headmaster Christopher Welsh, Foundation Day 1998 (The Oxleyan Vol. XVI, 1998, p.14)

2001

Construction of the Design and Technology building, the Oxley Foundation was established to receive donations and bequests for investment, and a Ball and Art and Fine Craft Exhibition were held.

2002

Inaugural Oxley Equestrian Day held at *Araluen*, the property of the Roche family, on a frosty Sunday in August. The day included ring events, dressage, show jumping and cross country.

2003

20th Anniversary of Oxley College. The theme of the celebrations was 'Building on the Past, Looking to the Future.' Opening of the PE Centre (now the Peter Craig Centre) and the Oxley Shop. Formerly the Clothing Pool, it was a Parents and Friends Association initiative, as was the new canteen.

Visitors to the College often comment on its immediate impact upon them. They speak of energy, a sense of purpose, of welcome and even of calm. Those of us who live the daily experience of the College know its imperfections, the blemishes that require a distinct response, not only to right the wrong but to offer young people (and the rest of us too) an opportunity to learn from error. Oxley's commitment to education of the whole person will therefore remain at its heart. We reaffirm that education of the mind and the body do not happen in a vacuum. They call also for education in values and of the human spirit, of the emotions and the conscience.

Headmaster Christopher Welsh, Speech Night 2003

Music Centre Appeal
A programme to fund the construction of a new specialist building for Music

Head's Report 2003

Strategic Plan

2004

Oxley College had 480 students, 45 teaching staff and 16 non-teaching staff.

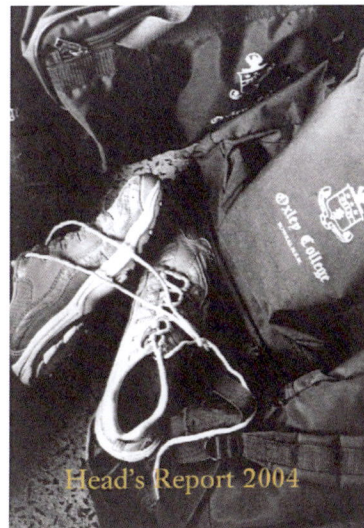

Head's Report 2004

During Oxley's annual Speech Night and prize giving ceremony, Oxley's Head of College customarily presents a summary of the school year. In his 2005 'Head's Report', Christopher Welsh identified three ways of learning at Oxley: learning in the classroom, learning outside the classroom and learning to live together in the community. Michael Parker (Headmaster 2014–2018) later expressed this as the enduring and evocative phrase, 'To Think, To Dare, To Dream'.

A few of the events, activities, accomplishments and achievements associated with Oxley College students and the broader school community over the last 17 years, since the publication of *A Lovingly Woven Tapestry, Oxley College Bowral 1983–2004* follow. It is by no means a complete collection, that would require several books – rather, it is a glimpse and reflection on the continuing life of Oxley College.

2005

Oxley's new Music Centre was opened on the evening of Friday 26 August, with festivities continuing over the weekend. Music students in all year groups performed and events included a Fine Arts Exhibition, opened by John Olsen AO, OBE, and a concert by the Macquarie Trio chamber music ensemble.

On Foundation Day, the Chairman of Governors Brian Hanrahan, announced that although he would remain on the Board, he would not be seeking re-election as Chair. Mr Hanrahan had been a Governor for 17 years and Chairman for six years when the announcement was made. Head of College, Christopher Welsh, said 'His contribution has been exceptional, and the College owes him a substantial debt of thanks for his leadership'.*

Other Board changes saw the retirement of Governor Dr John Pritchard, after 13 years. Dr Pritchard's contribution was an untiring commitment to capital development as Chairman of the Building Committee. He supervised the refurbishment of the Art Cottage, construction of the changerooms, the canteen and covered area, the replacement of the roof on the De La Salle building, the refurbishment of the laboratories, the Design and Technology facilities, the David Wright Library, the PE Centre and the Music School. Of Dr Pritchard's retirement Mr Welsh said, 'He has always worked hard to balance the imperatives of design with financial restraint, and the buildings we enjoy are testimony to his thoroughness and hard work.'†

* Head's comment, Weekly Record, 27 May 2005
† ibid

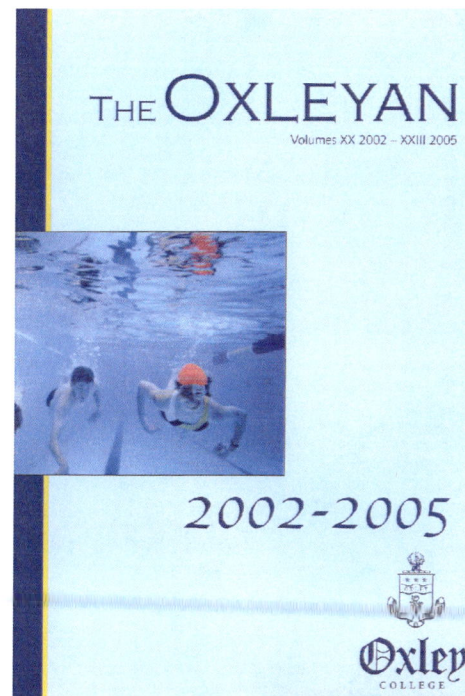

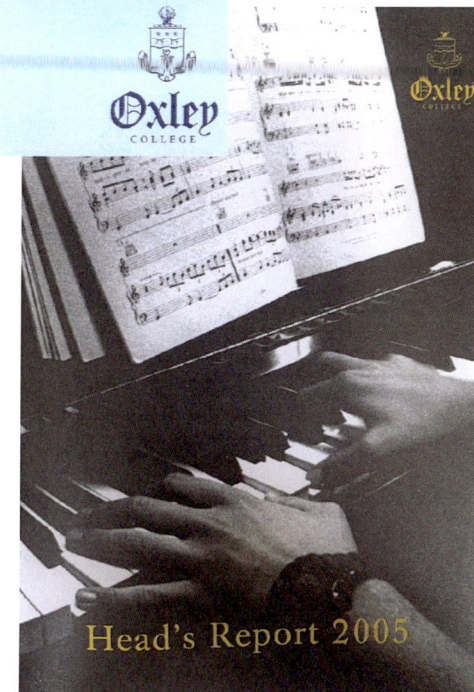

CHRISTOPHER JAMES WELSH

Head of Oxley College 1995–2008

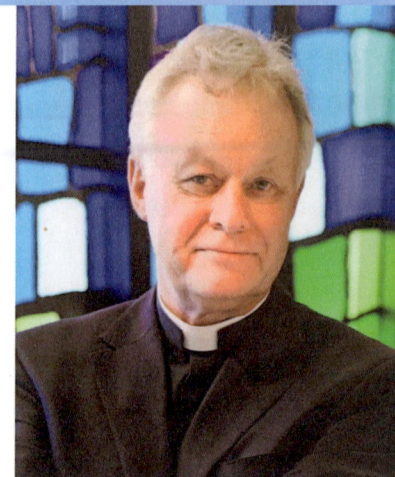

Chris Welsh was born in 1946 in England, where he received his early education at Laleham Church of England School and Hampton Grammar School. In 1968 he graduated with honours from St David's College, University of Wales, majoring in French, German and Biblical Studies. After two years teaching French and German at Llandovery County High School in Wales, in 1970 he was appointed Head of Languages and later Head of the Humanities Division at the Phoenix School in Telford, Shropshire.

Seeking to broaden his horizons, he arrived in Australia with his family in 1975 to take up the appointment of Senior French Teacher at Frensham. During his 10 years at Frensham, in addition to teaching and pastoral care as the Year 10 Form Master, he was extensively involved in drama and musical productions within the school and progressively took on additional roles in which he was able to offer advice to the Headmistress and Board of Governors.

In 1985 Chris Welsh became the fourth Head of Northholm Grammar School at Arcadia, an independent co-educational school founded in 1983. During his 10 year incumbency, the school grew to full enrolment of 460 students and established itself as a reputable and successful educational community, known for academic integrity, broad co-curricular programs and a strong emphasis on pastoral care. With the increase in the school population came the responsibility for considerable capital development works and growth in educational programs and staffing, experience that would prove to be of immense value when he was appointed Head of Oxley College in 1995.

His postgraduate studies at the University of New England led to the degree of Master of Education, with a particular research interest in the field of values education and theology. In 2001 he was awarded a Graduate Diploma in Theology from Charles Sturt University. Chris has been vitally involved in the various associations and advisory bodies of his profession. He has served as a member of many committees, including the Association of Heads of Independent Schools of Australia (AHISA), of which he served as Chair, State Chair, Chairman of the Social Issues Committee and as a member of the National Standing Committee. After more than 12 years at Oxley which saw the College come of age and develop educationally and in its facilities, Chris resigned to take Holy Orders and an appointment at Canberra Grammar School as Chaplain, where he served for more than eight years. In 2010 he was appointed Headmaster and Rector to guide the school through a period of transition until the arrival of a new Head. During that time he was a member of the Diocesan Schools Council in the Diocese of Canberra and Goulburn and undertook work leading retreats for school leaders in Sydney, Perth and Adelaide.

Never the retiring type, Chris graduated from full-time employment in 2016. He and wife Deborah have taken a number of locum appointments in Canberra, Lisbon, Lausanne, Gilbralter, Geneva and Milan within the Diocese in Europe. Chris also assists in a local community, Iona Anglicans, based in Sutton Forest. His interests are wide and include music, theatre, cricket, outdoor pursuits and cooking.

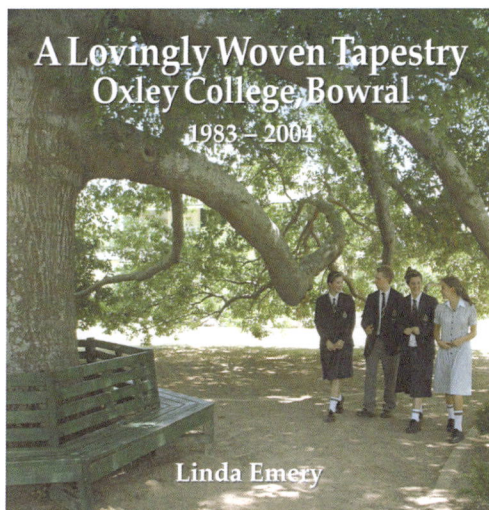

Launch of the book *A Lovingly Woven Tapestry, Oxley College Bowral, 1983–2004*, written by author and historian Linda Emery, a former Oxley Governor and parent. A digital version of the book is available to download by scanning the QR code on the last page of this book.

New sports uniform introduced with students permitted, for the first time, to arrive at school in sports uniform every Wednesday – the school's sports day.

In pre-NAPLAN years, the Commonwealth Government required Year 7 students to sit SNAP tests (Secondary Numeracy Assessment Program). This testing program was a condition of receiving funding support from the Government.

Drama productions – *A Chorus Line*, written by Michael Bennett, directed by Phil Cunich; *A Doll's House* by Henrik Ibsen, directed by Robert Graham.

Astronomer, Professor Fred Watson AM, presented the second Oxley Lecture, titled 'Big telescopes for a small world.' The Oxley Lectures were designed to enrich the intellectual and cultural life of the College and the local community and the evenings attracted a large and varied audience. The third Oxley Lecture was delivered by James Woodford, an author and science and environment writer.

The annual AHISA (Association of Heads of Independent Schools of Australia) conference was held at Oxley during August, with representatives from 80 schools attending.

Scene from A Chorus Line

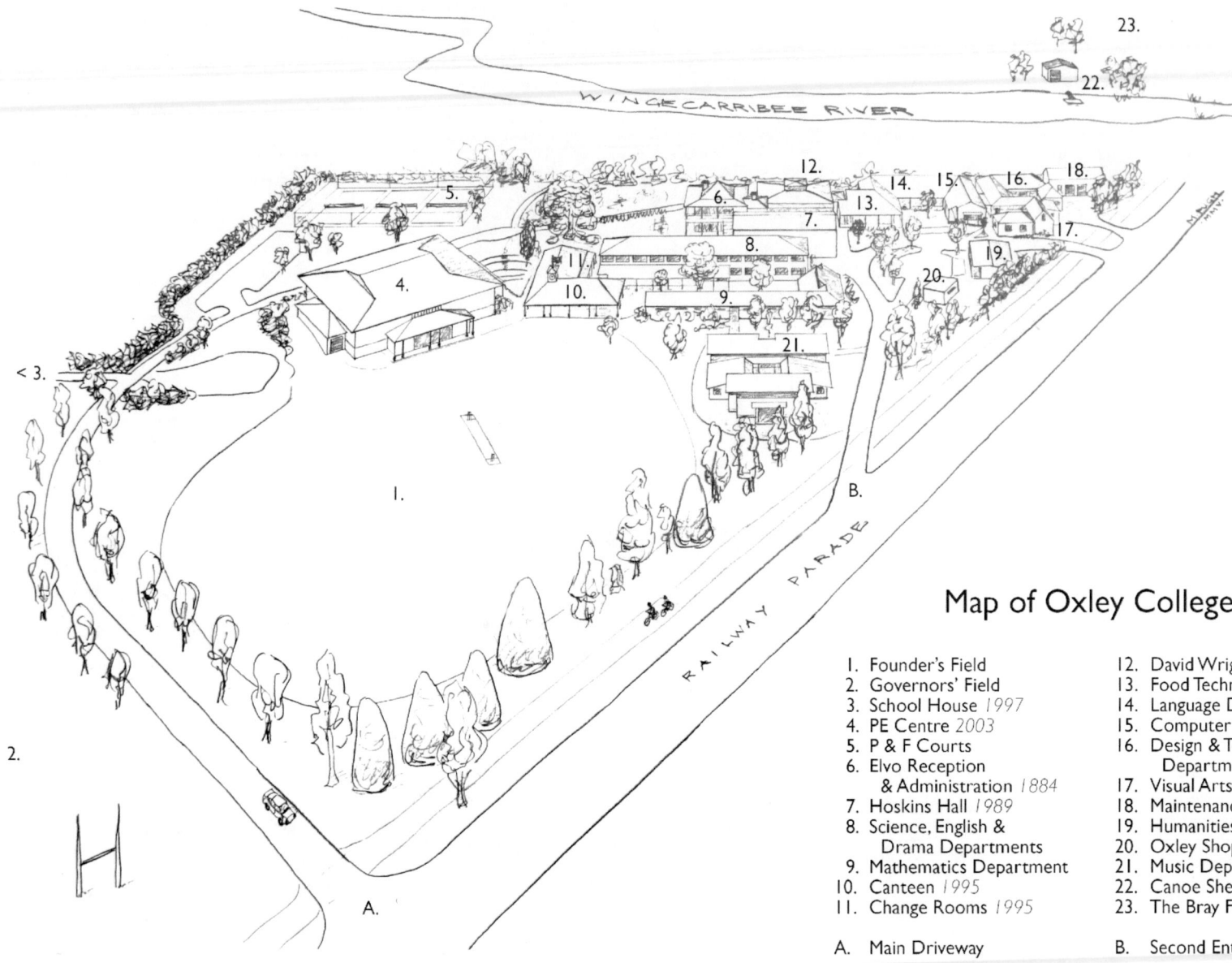

WINGECARRIBEE RIVER

Map of Oxley College

1. Founder's Field
2. Governors' Field
3. School House *1997*
4. PE Centre *2003*
5. P & F Courts
6. Elvo Reception
   & Administration *1884*
7. Hoskins Hall *1989*
8. Science, English &
   Drama Departments
9. Mathematics Department
10. Canteen *1995*
11. Change Rooms *1995*

12. David Wright Library *1996*
13. Food Technology
14. Language Department
15. Computer Department
16. Design & Technology
    Department
17. Visual Arts Department
18. Maintenance Area
19. Humanities Department
20. Oxley Shop *2003*
21. Music Department *2005*
22. Canoe Shed
23. The Bray Fields

A. Main Driveway

B. Second Entrance

RAILWAY PARADE

2005 Map of Oxley College created by Michael Pugh

The opening of the Music School was simple and effective and this sense of people centeredness flowed through into John Olsen's opening of the Art Exhibition. He picked up very quickly on the mood of Oxley, it's 'feel' which he described as 'democratic'. It was, he said, evident both from the people he encountered and from the facilities and the architecture.

'Head's Comment', Weekly Record, 2 September 2005

Duncan Webber and Hannah Stanton (Year 11) represented the College at the national Model United Nations Assembly (MUNA) in Canberra. Under the guidance of Mr Schaefer the Oxley team represented East Timor and were awarded the Frank Totenhoffer Peace Shield, for the country to best represent world peace at MUNA.

Parents and Friends Association events included a Regency themed costume ball and the Bray Fields to Berrima dash, a social kayaking event. In February the Parents and Friends Association presented $38,000 to the College in support of the construction of the Music Centre. This was in addition to $83,000 donated at the end of 2004.

Musicians from Gippsland Grammar School visited for a workshop and concert and were hosted by Oxley families.

Oxleyan Sarah Barrett played centre for the Sydney Swifts in the National Netball final and Alex Kanaar (Class of 2000) was selected to play in the Wallabies Under 21 Rugby Team. Wallabies coach Eddie Jones gave the First XV and 16s Rugby teams a training session at Eridge Park.

Joe Slowiaczek (Year 11) achieved outstanding success at several national and international Fencing competitions, qualifying as a competitor in the 2006 Commonwealth Games.

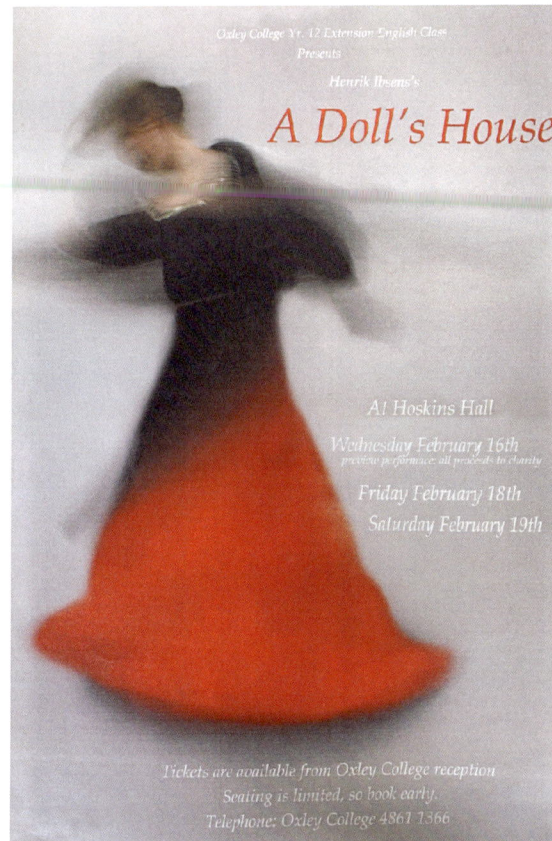

Oxley College Yr. 12 Extension English Class
Presents
Henrik Ibsen's's
A Doll's House

At Hoskins Hall
Wednesday February 16th
preview performance: all proceeds to charity
Friday February 18th
Saturday February 19th

Tickets are available from Oxley College reception
Seating is limited, so book early.
Telephone: Oxley College 4861 1366

The College must strive to cultivate young men and women of honesty and integrity, independence of mind, with the confidence and courage to stand against mediocrity, selfishness, and the standards of the day when these are seen to fall.

Headmaster Christopher Welsh, referring to Oxley's Statement of Purpose and Principal in 'Head's Comment', Weekly Record, 23 September 2005

MURRAY WALKER OAM (1930–2018)

Oxley Board of Governors 2001–2013
Chairman 2005–2009

Murray Walker was very proud of Oxley. He attended Foundation Night and Speech Night every year. Oxley has much to thank him for. He presided over Oxley at a time of its great good health. He was both an enthusiast and a gentleman.

However, Oxley was only a part of his life and for a short amount of time. One of his most enduring life's passions was sailing and being on the water. During World War II he lived near Sydney Harbour and when the US warships came into Sydney Harbour he would take his sailing dinghy out with a friend. Not content to simply look at the warships, they would deliberately capsize his boat as close as possible to the ships and pretend that they were in strife. The generous US sailors would then drag Murray and his friend aboard and give him a piece of the American chewing gum that he loved. He sailed for many years. As an adult he also competed in a multitude of races in a variety of craft. He worked in advertising and was responsible for many significant accounts with many highly regarded firms. He became a Fellow of the Advertising Institute of Australia.

Murray also made his mark in the wide variety of charity and honorary positions that he held. Not least of these was Chairman of the Royal Sydney Golf Club for five years. He was also the Commodore of the Prince Edward Yacht Club and sat on both the 1988 Sydney Olympic Games Committee and the Sydney Symphony Orchestra Committee, was a Director of the Foundation for the National Parks and Wildlife Service, (Taronga and Western Plains Zoos) and he was a Foundation Member of the National Seniors Association. He contributed to the Key

Committee for the Multiple Sclerosis Society and worked for youth with a drug addiction through his role as a Director of the Odyssey House Drug Remedial Programme. It was therefore not a surprise when he was awarded a Medal of the Order of Australia (OAM).

Murray sadly passed away in August 2018 and many people spoke in their eulogies at his memorial service at St Jude's in Bowral, of the importance of family in his life. He was father to Simon, Jane, Sophie and Charles and grandfather to Toby, Anouk, Alastair, Hugh and Victoria. He also leaves behind his first wife Shirley and his second wife of almost 60 years, artist Mandy Walker.

In recognition of Murray's love and support of visual arts, Oxley College created the Murray Walker Art Prize for a Year 12 artwork to be hung in the *Elvo* reception area for five years. His commitment and passion for Oxley was remarkable and his legacy is significant. He also delighted in seeing his grandchildren's various journeys through the College.

"The College aims to develop in its students a spiritedness and sensitivity in all they do, think and feel. I would like, particularly, to say this to you students, that after your years at Oxley, you will carry into adulthood an understanding of your own unique gifts, a sense of challenge, an acceptance of your responsibilities, and an awareness and understanding of the needs of others."

Murray Walker, Chairman, Board of Governors, Speech Night 2008

2006

Inaugural Hoskins Concert held in the Orchestra Room of the new Music Centre, featuring performances by the College's ensemble groups and HSC Music students.

Art Camp held at Biloela where students created ephemeral artworks insired by nature.

Primatologist and anthropologist Dr Jane Goodall visited Oxley. Students joined Dr Goodall's 'Roots and Shoots' program, a global network of young people taking action to improve the world for people, animals and the environment. The program's mission includes fostering respect and compassion for all living things and promoting understanding of all cultures and beliefs.

Inaugural visit by Dutch English-language students from KSG Apeldoorn, a school 100km east of Amsterdam. The visit was arranged by Peter Craig, Director of International Programs, to celebrate the 400th anniversary of the Dutch exploration of the Gulf of Carpentaria by William Jansz in a small sailing ship, the Dyfken (Little Dove). Teacher Nick Wansey and six Oxley students later visited KSG Apeldoorn and Tilburg in the Netherlands, to take part in further celebrations of Australian and Dutch relations. Reciprocal annual visits between students of Oxley and KSG Apeldoorn took place for about 16 years. The Dutch students and staff were billeted with Oxley families during their visit.

Right: Geography students on excursion

Above: Interhouse tug-of-war competition held on the annual Mission Day

Right: Happy Equestrian Day participants

In Drama, *The Silver Sword*, a dramatisation by Stuart Henson of Ian Serraillier's 1956 novel, was staged over six nights in May and June. Head of English, Robert Graham, directed a cast and crew of over 40 students from Years 7–12 in the production, set during World War II. In his Director's Note for the play's program, Robert Graham wrote:

> Rehearsals have been going on since the beginning of Term 1. Hundreds of hours have been spent in thinking and planning even before that, drawing, model building, costume making, set building and painting, organising and making props, hanging and focusing lights, photographing, advertising, poster making, ticketing, arranging, interval refreshments, front of house, make-up and hairdressing …
>
> Polished productions do not grow on trees. They are the marriage of talent, hard work and dedication. All of us involved have lived with this show for months – it has become part of us. The Silver Sword has not been easy, far from it, but it is a good example of what a collective will and understanding can achieve.

The *Silver Sword* won four awards at the 2007 Canberra Area Theatre (CAT) Awards, including Best Production of a school or youth play. Duncan Webber (Year 12) was awarded Best Actor, Robert Lloyd won Best Set Design and Oxley parent Joy Burgess won Best Costume Design. Joy designed and constructed costumes for hundreds of Oxley students between 1995 and 2008. The Joy Burgess Costume Room was named as a tribute to her. After the play was finished, Joy received the following note from Duncan Webber:

> Dear Mrs Burgess,
>
> You have been the person that has made so many Oxley productions look the way they do. You are a slave driver and a tyrant in the dressing room, but all your efforts are appreciated.
>
> This being my last production, I realise what an effect you have had. I will not forget your costumes anytime soon.
>
> Sincerely, D. Webber

Never refuse to tread a path that you think you cannot conquer, as you may surprise yourself, either in the short term or later in life. Always fear regret.

Dr Nicholas Coupe (class of 1996) Old Oxleyan Foundation Day speech 2006

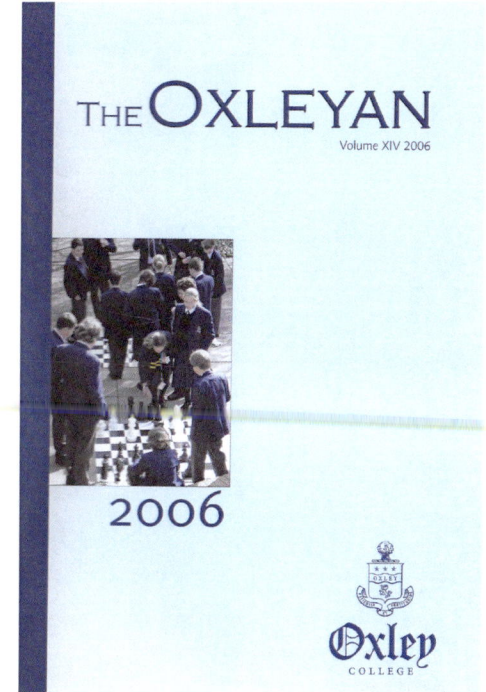

THE OXLEYAN

Volume XIV 2006

2006

Oxley
COLLEGE

Watercolour self-portraits by Year 11 Art students, Gavin Shaw, Vivienne Grant and Zoe Burgess selected for an exhibition at the National Portrait Gallery in Canberra.

Oxley Cricket tour to Ireland, Scotland and England.

The play *A Christmas Carol* was performed by Oxley students, staff and professional local actors to raise funds for the children's ward at Bowral Hospital. Directed by Dave Letch it was the second year the group staged the classic tale by Charles Dickens. The Oxley College Choir performed as part of the show.

Above: Equestrian Day

Right: Oxley cricket players with teachers Tim Dibdin and Peter Craig at Frensham Cricket Club in England, the Dibdin family's local club with father, brother and Tim all playing there.

Far right: Scene from The Silver Sword

Above: Outback

... as Old Oxleyans get together, they find themselves asking each other 'Did you go on Outback?' – so a common thread has bound the year groups together in a very unique way, and the secret can be shared from 1988 until today.

Annik Schaefer, A Lovingly Woven Tapestry

Above: Staff (left to right) Tim Dibdin, Helmut Schaefer, Randa Warda, Ros Hamilton, David McGuiness, Trish Topp and Peter Freeman

Left: Students relaxing on Founder's Field

Below: A happy admin team sharing coffee at the old Student Services (currently Mark Case's office). Left to right: Lorrae Mueller, Linda Garwood, Yvonne Thomas, Judy Loydstrom, Beverley Harris and Joanne Richards. Yvonne and Beverley worked at Oxley for more than 20 years, as have Lorrae and Joanne, who are still there as at 2023.

2007

Head of College Christopher Welsh resigned from Oxley after more than 12 years to take up the position of Chaplain at Canberra Grammar School. Grant Williamson was appointed to replace him and commenced at the start of 2008.

Inaugural 'Back to Oxley Day' for Old Oxleyans.

New Staff Common Room opened.

Elvo reception area improved to accommodate display of student artworks.

Major Drama production *Cabaret*, performed by more than 50 students and a seven piece student band.

A Japanese language class was introduced and three Oxley students studying French participated in a language exchange program with French students studying English.

Rugby Opens Squad tour to New Zealand.

Teachers Phil Cunich, Rob Hughes and Kate Cunich accompanied a group of Oxley musicians to China on their first international tour.

Schools are not glossy places. They deal with the everyday challenges and ups and downs of apprentice human beings. We recognise, those of us who think about it, that there is no greater work. We are laying the foundations of a future, our future as individuals, as a society, a nation, and a civilization. It is hard, demanding work.

Headmaster Christopher Welsh, Foundation Day 2007

At Oxley, one never hears the expression: 'Oh, it's only a school play …'.

Robert Graham

Left: Teacher Peter Craig and Year 8 History students during the annual Medieval Feast

Opposite: A scene from Cabaret

Oxley Snowsports team relax in the snow

Outback group with Helmut Schaefer and Stuart Forlonge

This page: Students on Visual Arts Camp

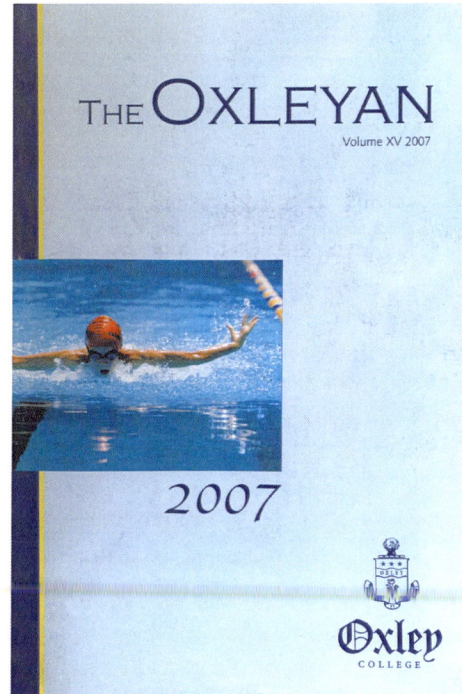

VALE

On 6 May a memorial service was held for Oxley parent John Stanton in the Oxley PE Centre (now the Peter Craig Centre). Attended by more than 800 people, Head of College Chris Welsh said it was only fitting that the celebration of John's life was held in 'the house that John built', as he was 'substantially instrumental' in its construction. Speaking at the service Mr Welsh said:

We all know how John was enormously generous, generous with what he had at his disposal but above all, generous of spirit. He brought his trucks, his machines and his men, and quietly shifted tens of thousands of tonnes of fill from this site and just as quietly dumped it over there to extend the playing fields. He used to sit or stand in here and look up and get that quiet sense of excitement from having been a part of it. He was like that.

John and Karen Stanton's five children, Emily, Hannah, Oliver, Patrick and Spencer attended Oxley between 1998 and 2015.

THOMAS 'GRANT' WILLIAMSON

Head of Oxley College 2008–2014

Grant was raised in a rural community in Western Australia and moved to New South Wales in the early 1980s. After his appointment as Oxley's Head of College in 2007, Grant and wife Margaret relocated to the Southern Highlands, where he found the people in the area were similar to where he was from – a strong, close and supportive community.

During his tenure as Head of College, Grant is most proud of the opening of the Junior School in 2012, after four years of intensive planning and building. Of this process Grant said, 'It took a few years to pull it together, but it would not have occurred at all without the foresight and wonderful leadership, support and guidance of the Board. They imagined what the future of the school might look like and provided the opportunities to make it happen.'

Not long after Grant arrived at Oxley in 2008 the world entered a global financial crisis, the most serious and stressful economic crisis since the Great Depression of 1929–1939. Grant described this period as 'a bit difficult to navigate', and acknowledged that the assistance of Beverley Harris, Oxley's long term business manager at the time, was 'absolutely fantastic.'*

On the academic side, Grant introduced the Visible Learning methodology to the school whereby students are taught to identify what they need to learn, how to learn it and how to evaluate their own progress. He said, 'At the time there was a huge focus on improving outcomes for kids in the classroom and we devoted a lot of time to Visible Learning and the results were very good.'

He also worked closely with Principals from other Independent and State schools in the area and found the sharing of knowledge and ideas contributed towards a mutual goal of achieving better educational outcomes for the whole community.

Grant's extra-curricular activities in the Southern Highlands included volunteering with the Berrima District NSW Rural Service. He was also part of the Wingecarribee Shire School/Business Community Partnership program and a member of the Alternate Learning Centre, Local Enabling Group and Youth Hub steering committee.

Prior to his appointment as Head of Oxley College, Grant had many wide ranging senior leadership, academic, teaching, pastoral and co-curricular roles, at Guildford Grammar School at Guildford, east of Perth and later at Newington College in Sydney, between 1984–2007.

After leaving Oxley in April 2014 Grant worked with educational organisations at Pathways International Consulting, moved to Brisbane, Queensland and was the Assistant Director of School Services at Independent Schools Queensland (ISQ). Grant also established TGW Investments: Grant Williamson Consulting and Executive Coaching, providing support for organisations and individuals. The consultancy offers services to clients in the areas of governance, coaching and operations. He is also an Executive Advisor with the Executive Master of Business Administration (EMBA) at the Queensland University Business School of Technology.

*Grant Williamson, Former Head of College, speaking at Foundation Day assembly 2022

2008

Grant Williamson commenced as Head of College.

Oxley College Alumni website launched by Peter Craig. Facebook is now used by Old Oxleyans to share information and stay in touch.

Geography students and teachers traveled to Sabah in Malaysian Borneo and were the first guests to stay at the Tungog Rainforest Eco-Camp. Students visited the Sepilok Orangutan Sanctuary, the Sandakan War Memorial in Kota Kinabalu and assisted with forest restoration, planting 300 native trees.

Oxley Cricket tour to England, Holland and Singapore. In Holland the group were hosted by Dutch School KSG Apeldoorn, who visited Oxley earlier in the year.

Year 12 English teachers from 35 schools in the Southern Highlands and the Illawarra attended a professional learning event at Oxley, in collaboration with the Association of Independent Schools.

Inaugural Southern Highlands HSC Music Composition Day organised by Oxley's Head of Music, Robert Hughes. Over 100 senior Music students from local schools and the HICES network attended the intensive workshop.

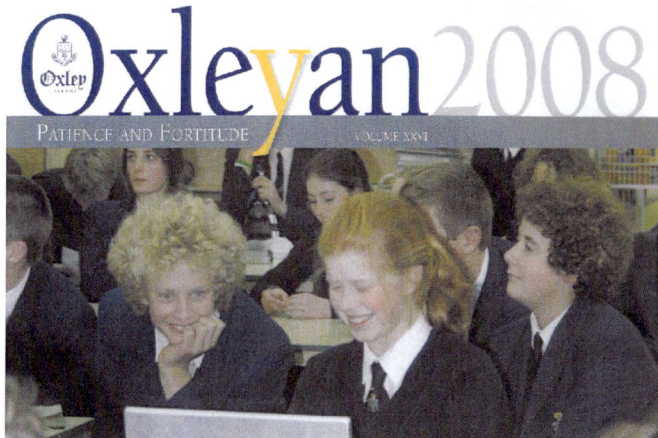

Oxleyan 2008
PATIENCE AND FORTITUDE   VOLUME XXVI

Head's Report 2008

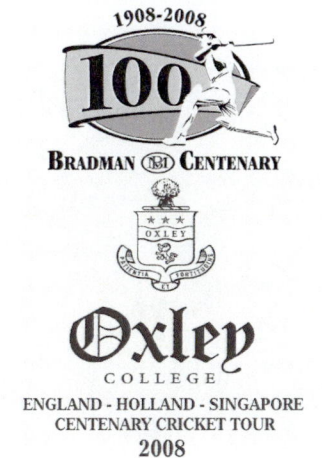

1908-2008
100
BRADMAN CENTENARY
OXLEY
Oxley
COLLEGE
ENGLAND - HOLLAND - SINGAPORE
CENTENARY CRICKET TOUR
2008

This page: Scenes from Macbeth

Opposite: Scenes from Grimm Tales

Oxley is known for producing theatrical performances of a very high standard and quality. Year after year successful productions are staged in Hoskins Hall to capacity audiences. The Senior Drama production in 2008 was Shakespeare's *Macbeth*. Directed by Paul Gardiner, the striking costumes (leather and armour) were made by parent Joy Burgess.

In the Year 7–10 production of *Grimm Tales*, 83 students were cast in the various plays within a play. Year 11 Drama students acted as assistant directors. The costumes were designed by Oxley parent Lucinda Dazos. Working closely with Drama teacher Phil Cunich, Lucinda designed costumes for Oxley Drama productions for an incredible 29 years. Also a wonderful chef, Lucinda has cooked and catered for countless Oxley functions and events over the last twenty or so years. Lucinda and her late husband Nick Dazos's sons, Arthur, Michael and Marcus, attended Oxley between 2001 and 2014.

The inaugural Oxley Playwriting Festival was held in May and at the 2008 Fast and Fresh Festival, Jack Munro won Best Actor for his performance in *Cluedo*, by Matt Perger. In another highlight for the year in performing arts, Year 12 student Ellie Mackay achieved 98% in HSC Drama, placing her 6th in New South Wales, the third time an Oxley student had featured in the top 10 in New South Wales for Drama.

HICES Music Festival and camp at Stanwell Tops attended by 10 Oxley students across Years 7–12.

Year 11 Art Camp held at Biloela Outdoor Education facility. Inspired by their teacher Ms Lampert, students wore white overalls and inscribed them with quotes from artists and philosophers. Their overalls and photographs of their environmental art featured in the annual HSC Art Exhibition. Wonderful environmental art installations were also created around the school.

Exchange students from Kaifeng Senior Middle School in China visited Oxley as part of an exchange between Wingecarribee Shire and Kaifeng. The visiting students were hosted by Oxley and Frensham families.

About 60 former students and Brothers of De La Salle College attended a reunion held at Oxley on 20 September. The De La Salle Brothers purchased *Elvo* in 1959 and established a secondary school for boys who wished to enter the priesthood. Memories were shared of cold winter evenings, studying in temporary classrooms in the stable building (now the Art Centre) eating in the dining room (College reception) and singing in the Chapel – the Head of College office.

Several fundraising events were organised by students to raise money for the Multiple Sclerosis Society. The Oxley Staff Bike Ride team joined the efforts, participating in the MS Sydney to Wollongong bike ride (90 kms). Student Jess Sheaffe was diagnosed with MS during 2008 and spoke at a school assembly with courage and wisdom. More than $11,500 was raised by the Oxley community.

Right: Students on Art Camp. Opposite: Senior Chemistry students

VALE

Donald Geoffrey Hoskins (1917–2008) Founding Chairman of Oxley College Board of Governors 1982–1987. A Memorial Service for Mr Hoskins was held in Hoskins Hall on 5 May 2008.

Donald Hoskins was a retired engineer and company director whose administrative ability extended beyond the business sphere to his previous membership of the Annesley School Board and involvement with SCEGGS at Moss Vale. In *A Lovingly Woven Tapestry* Linda Emery wrote:

Don's business experience, negotiating skills and wisdom were vital in ensuring that Oxley College became a reality. Always supporting her husband and the College, Betty Hoskins, too, played an important role in the life of the school. Her shining personality and genuine interest in the development of Oxley made her one of the College's most outstanding ambassadors. In 1987 Don Hoskins was honoured by Headmaster David Wright in a succinct appraisal of this outstanding leader.

The one who has guided the College with great wisdom and great love, the one who has contributed more to its establishment than anyone could ever imagine, the one who has been mentor, guide, leader, supporter, friend; the one without whom I have often believed it doubtful whether there would ever have been an Oxley at all, is presiding at his last speech day. On behalf of the whole Oxley family, I thank Don Hoskins and his wife Betty for a remarkable job done for the College.

Don and Betty Hoskins

VALE

Matthew Boatwright, 'Boaty' (1991–2008) Year 11 student and member of Dobell House who tragically died following a car accident during the July school holidays. A plaque at the school in Matthew's memory reads 'A day without laughter is a day wasted.'

Far left: Christopher Welsh's portrait was hung in the David Wright library. Present for the unveiling were Grant Williamson, Mandy and Murray Walker, Betty and Peter Bray, artist Dave Thomas and (seated) Betty and Don Hoskins.

Left: All Schools National Fencing Tournament champions Max Peek, Nick Davies and John Downes. It was the team's second national title and the fourth for Oxley in five years. In 2009 John Downes won medals at the Youth Olympic Festival and the Junior Commonwealth Fencing Championships in Malaysia.

Below left: Landcare activities included redeveloping a native wetland area next to the Music Centre the native garden outside the Music Centre. A pond was dug with an excavator and modelled further with picks and shovels, mostly by Year 8 students, who also planted many new wetland species.

Below: Staff and former students on Foundation Day.

2009

The year began against a background of uncertainty, as the global financial crisis adversely affected economic conditions in Australia. During Speech Night, Oxley's new Chairman Frank Conroy AM assured the Oxley community that, 'Overall, the College is in a sound financial position and more than capable of meeting the challenges of the future.'

There were several changes to the Board of Governors during the year. Murray Walker OAM stood down as Chairman at the Annual General Meeting and Frank Conroy was elected to replace him. Martin Lemann retired as a Governor after 12 years on the Board and six years as a consultant. Among his various roles he was Chairman of the Building Committee and a member of the Finance Committee. In commending his long and close association with Oxley, Murray Walker described Martin as being '... part of the very backbone of Oxley.' Marie Fitzpatrick also stepped down from the Board in 2009, after eight years of strong and valued contribution.

There were 40 editions of the *Weekly Record* newsletter published during the year. A vital communication tool, the *Weekly Record* kept the Oxley community informed of school matters for many years.

Oxley's Outdoor Education program changed its name to OLE (Other Learning Experiences). OLE provides opportunities for students to participate in enriching activities beyond the classroom with an active, community or cultural focus.

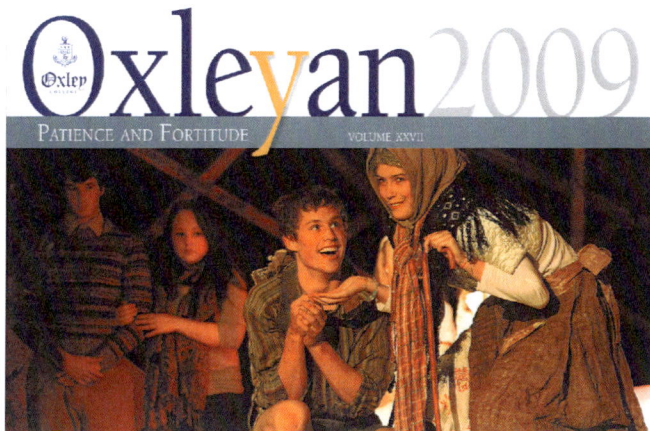

The task of teaching students to think well and to think critically forms a baseline for education at Oxley. The Board, the Head of College, our wonderful staff and the Parents and Friends are all involved as one community to help our students achieve this end.

Murray Walker OAM, Chairman's Speech Foundation Day

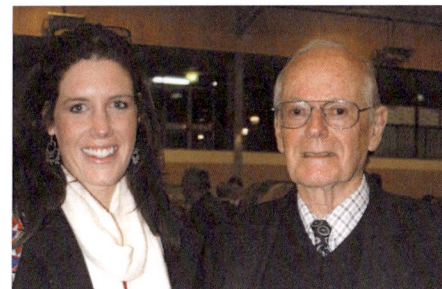

Left: Martin Lemann with former student Hollie Baillieu at an Oxley function

FRANK J CONROY AM

Oxley Board of Governors 2008–2020
Chairman 2009–2020

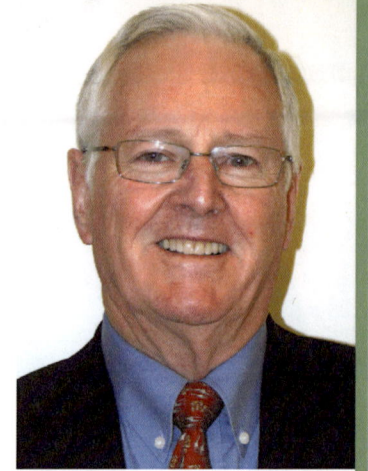

Born and raised in Perth, Western Australia, an unsuccessful application to attend Teachers' College led to Frank joining the Bank of New South Wales at a small branch in Perth. He was appointed a country branch manager in 1972 and transferred to Head Office in Sydney in 1975.

Frank remained with Westpac Banking Corporation for 32 years, serving in several branch and executive management positions in Australia, the United Kingdom and Hong Kong. He resigned from the position of Chief Executive Officer and Managing Director in December 1992 and until his retirement from active corporate life in 2004, Frank served as a company director on public companies and government boards. In 1993, he was appointed by the Federal Government as Chairman of the Committee to review the Australian Customs Service.

Frank was introduced to Oxley College by former Governor, the late Martin Lemann when Oxley College was seeking an alternate banker. He joined the Board of Governors in June 2008 following a request from the Chairman, the late Murray Walker OAM, and became Chairman in May 2009. He stepped down from the Board of Governors in May 2020 to comply with the College Constitution's prescribed maximum term of twelve years. There were three Heads of College during Frank's tenure on the Board, Grant Williamson, Michael Parker and Jenny Ethell.

The public companies with which Frank served included St. George Bank Ltd. (Chairman), Howard Smith Ltd. (Chairman), Orix Australia Corporation Ltd., (Chairman), Australian Pharmaceutical Industries Ltd. (Chairman), Elders Australia Ltd. (Chairman), Santos Ltd., Davids Ltd., Placer Pacific Ltd., Futuris Corporation Ltd., Bank of Tokyo Australia Ltd., M2 Motorway Bidding Syndicate (Chairman), Westpac Banking Corporation and Placer Pacific Staff Superannuation Pty. Ltd. (Chairman).

Government boards and organizations included Federal Airports Corporation (Chairman), Tourism Forecasting Council (Chairman), N.S.W. Committee for the Australia Remembers Program (Chairman), Australian Defence College, Australia-China Council and Royal Botanic Gardens and Domain Trust of N.S.W. He was a member of the South-Western Sydney Local Health District Board from 2012 to 2016 and has served on the Advisory Boards of P.A. Management Consulting, Allen Allen & Hemsley Solicitors and Philips Electronics Australia. Other interests have included the Australian Brandenburg Orchestra (Chairman), Air Training Corps National Council (Deputy Chairman), The Sydney Institute (Treasurer), Heart Foundation, University of Western Australia Hackett Foundation, Investment Committee of the Australian Club, and the Australian War Memorial–Sydney Fundraising Committee. From 2010 to 2016, he mentored senior executives of the banking and other industries.

Frank holds a Bachelor of Commerce from the University of Western Australia and a Master of Business Administration from Macquarie University. He is a Senior Fellow of the Financial Services Institute of Australasia, Fellow of the Institute of Managers and Leaders, and a Fellow of the Australian Institute of Company Directors. In 2014 he was appointed as a Member in the General Division of the Order of Australia, for significant service to the finance and banking sector, to corporate administration and to the arts, health, and secondary education. He was also a recipient of the Centenary Medal for his contribution to business. Married with two adult children, Frank lives in Bowral, not far from Oxley College.

Oxley Parents and Friends Association held its inaugural Earth Hour event, which included a party for about 200 guests, RevivART exhibition and competition, silent auction and live music. The College was transformed into a twinkling fairy land with tea lights lighting the garden paths. The evening raised over $11,000 for the school.

Drama productions were *Stories In The Dark*, by Debra Oswald, and *The Insect Play* by the Capek Brothers. At the State Finals of the Fast and Fresh Short Play Competition, Oliver Penn, Marcus Traill, Scott Lee, Gabriel Gurieff and Peter Booth won Best Production for their piece *Thank God You're Here*. Scott went on to become a professional actor.

Over 100 senior music students from more than ten schools attended an HSC Music Enrichment Day at Oxley, organised by Rob Hughes. Indian musician Sandip Burman also held traditional Indian classical music workshops at Oxley.

Oxley hosted the Board of Studies Regional Design and Technology exhibition, displaying the best 2008 HSC Design and Technology Projects.

Oxley received three awards at the inaugural Southern Highlands Foundation Philanthropy awards: Elliot Smith (Year 10) won Youth Philanthropist 2009 for his involvement with the Making a Difference Youth Committee (MAD Youth) and the Wingecarribee Youth Council; The Nixon Family (Harriet Nixon Year 8) won Philanthropy Family 2009, and Oxley College was Highly Commended for Philanthropic School 2009.

Earth hour event

60 EARTH HOUR

PARENTS & FRIENDS
Invite you to join them for the
Oxley Earth Hour™ Event
Saturday 28th March 7 - 10pm
(Earth Hour™ 8.30-9.30pm)
at Oxley College

BYO: Personal Lighting
PRIZE FOR MOST ORIGINAL LIGHTING - NO NAKED FLAMES
Silent auction - Junk Art Exhibition - Live Music
Tickets $35 p/h drinks & canapes inc. RSVP: 23 March

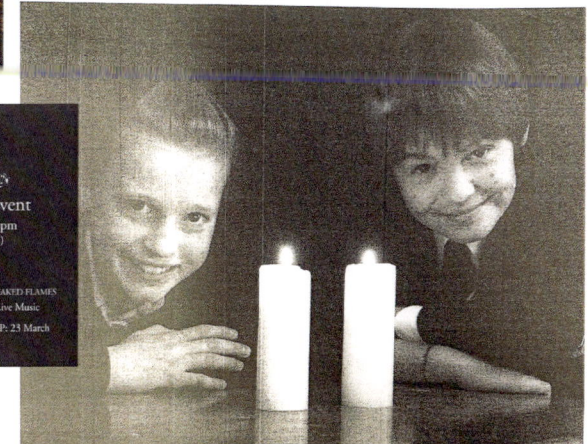

HighlandNews
THE HOME OF SIR DONALD BRADMAN
Wednesday, March 18, 2009
news online www.bowral.yourguide.com.au

HOPING FOR A BRIGHTER FUTURE: Year 7 Oxley College students Susannah Newton and William Maker get into the spirit of Earth Hour.   Photo by Robyn Murray

Kids to flick the switch

OXLEY College is joining communities across the world in switching off their lights for Earth Hour next Saturday, March 28.

More than 1000 towns and cities, from the Chatham Islands to the Arctic Sea, will turn off their lights between 8.30pm and 9.30pm in a call for definitive action on climate change.

Oxley College Parents and Friends (P&F) are inviting guests of their Earth Hour event to bring their own personal lighting, with a prize to be awarded for the most original.

P&F president Philip Chapman said Oxley College decided to support Earth Hour after the withdrawal of key sponsors forced the P&F to cancel its planned Eco Expo.

"We wanted to do something to make the community aware of the challenge to our planet," Mr Chapman said.

"We see it as something that we should all be aware of."

Oxley College's cocktail party-style Earth Hour event includes a junk art exhibition and silent auction with live music playing during the hour of darkness.

The junk art exhibition, sponsored by BDCU, will be open to the public on Sunday, March 29.

People who would like to take part in the Oxley Earth Hour should contact the college on 4861 1366 by March 23.

Earth Hour executive director Andy Ridley said Earth Hour is more than just a call to action on climate change.

"Earth Hour is an opportunity for the global community to speak in one voice on the issue of climate change, while at the same time coming together in celebration of the one thing every single person on the planet has in common - the planet," he said.

"Whether it's joining your community in a town square to watch the city lights go dark or hosting a lights-out party in your own home, I encourage everybody across the world to be a part of this historic occasion.

"Turn off your lights, celebrate the planet, enjoy the moment and cast your vote for Earth."

Students continued to assist Landcare Australia with restoration work along sections of the Wingecarribee River, in particular by removing pest willow trees from the river banks. Supported by the volunteer Willow Warriors organisation and assisted by a Caring for Country grant that helped supply equipment and provide safety measures, students on kayaks ventured into sometimes remote parts of the river and worked hard to clear willow trees from the river. It was also an ideal opportunity for Duke of Edinburgh students to achieve recognition for their community service.

Students collected over 100 obsolete mobile phones for the Cerebral Palsy Foundation's mobile phone recycling program.

Above: Scene from The Insect Play
Left: Student Visual Art work
Opposite: Year 10 students during the annual Australian Business Week event

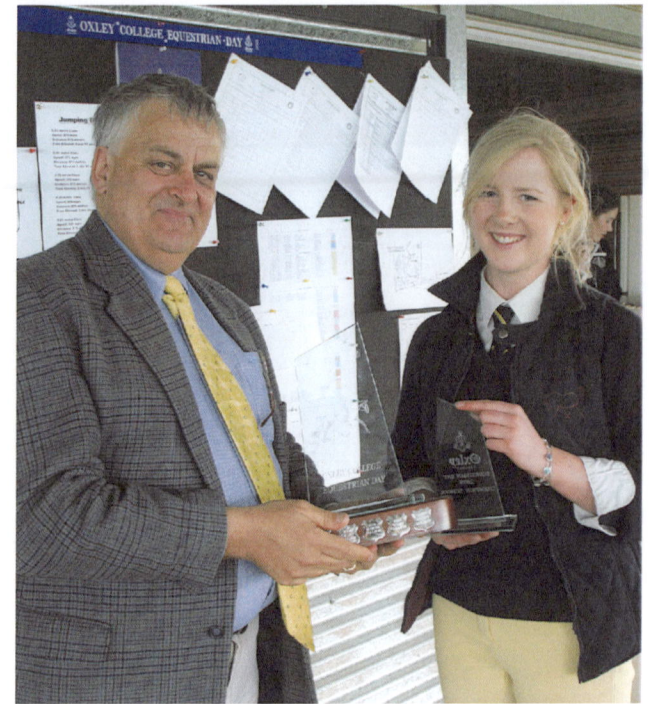

In Grant Williamson's second year at Oxley there was no let up in his endeavour to attend nearly every event and sporting fixture during the school year. He even attended the annual MS Head Shave, although he did not participate this year. He is seen here at Oxley's Equestrian Day and Swimming Carnival.

This was by far the best outdoor adventure I have ever been on. It has opened my eyes to the opportunities that are out there, all those places waiting to be explored and the 29,711 chances I have to do something new.

Discovering the Snowy Mountains, William Lawson, Year 10

Above and above left: Students surfing on the South Coast and hiking in the Snowy Mountains during OLE week

Sporting highlights were plentiful. To mention but a few, the Open B girls Basketball team and Junior A girls Softball team won their ISA Grand finals and Oxley won the shield for Most Successful School in Softball. Cricketer Stephen McNaught's name was engraved on the Oxley Century Cricket Bat after he scored an incredible 200 not out against Blue Mountains Grammar School on 5 December. Equestrians Edwina Hutton-Pots and Aiyana Levin represented NSW at the Equestrian Grand Nationals and Year 11 students Alex Syrros and Tom Young were selected for the Western Sydney representative AFL team in the U18 State competition. Tom was also selected to play with the NSW/ACT Rams team in the U18 Australian Championship. William Lawson played Rugby for Illawarra in the NSW Country Championships and was selected for the NSW Country squad. In Fencing, John Downes, Max Peek and Daniel Alchin (a former Oxley student) won medals at the Australian Youth Olympic Festival. John Downes also won silver and bronze medals in the Junior Commonwealth Fencing Championships in Malaysia.

The 2009 Student Representative Council

Above: Student Representative Council (SRC)
Right: The annual whole school disco

Elected by their peers, members of the SRC meet regularly to discuss matters of importance to students and make recommendations. The school community benefits from the engagement of students in decision making regarding the life of the College. Mission Day and the whole school disco are events held annually by the SRC. Money raised at these events is donated to student nominated charities.

Our students are the primary focus at Oxley College. We are here to help our students challenge themselves both inside and outside the classroom. Challenge themselves academically, in the creative, performing and spoken arts, in co-curricular and socially. Challenge them to continue to grow as an individual and strive to be the best they can. We exist to prepare our students, the young people in front of me, for their futures, whatever those futures may be. Our goal is to fully prepare the students entrusted to our care for the world in which they are likely to be living, so that they might live well, contribute fully to the society, and continue to learn and flourish in the path they take.

Grant Williamson, Head's Speech, Speech Night

2010

The covered Outdoor Learning Area was completed and landscaped, classrooms were painted and air-conditioning and ceiling fans were installed. The road that previously led up to *Elvo* was replaced with grass, a new office and seminar room were created in the library and the maintenance shed was extended.

In Drama, the Senior Production was *Evie & The Birdman*, an Australian musical written by John Field and directed by Phil Cunich. In the Junior Production, students from Years 7–10 filled 65 roles in Bertolt Brecht's sprawling classic, *The Caucasian Chalk Circle*. Set in pre-revolution Russia, Director Chris Canute said, 'Doing Brecht meant only one thing. We had to bring the Oxley Klezmer band on board. Mr Hodge and the band jumped at the opportunity and their enthusiasm for the project translated into a musical score that played a huge part in creating the world of the play.'* Also in Drama, two student plays were selected for the Fast & Furious Theatre State Finals and Peter Booth received the award for Best Director.

Three Oxley students were invited to attend an International Student Conference in Apeldoorn, in commemoration of Liberation Day (from Nazi occupation).

Rugby tour to New Zealand, followed by a Cricket tour to Barbados to play in the Sir Garfield Sobers International Schools Cricket Tournament. A legendary West Indian cricketer, Sir Garfield attended the event and met with the Oxley team.

*Co-Curricular Reports, *Oxleyan 2010*, p.43

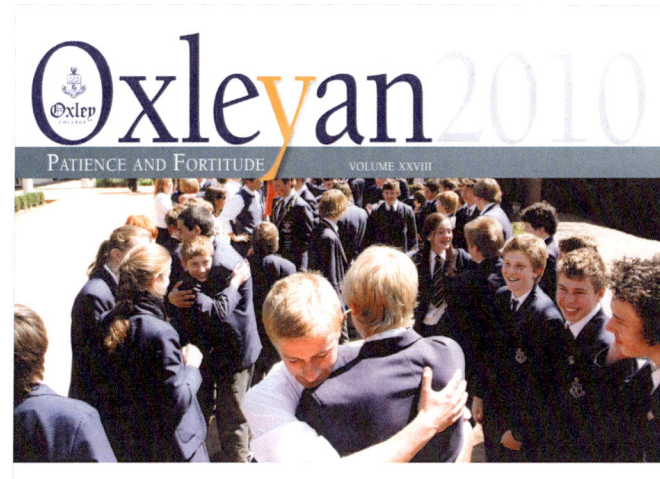

Scenes from The Caucasian Chalk Circle *(above) and* Evie and the Birdman *(right)*

Year 12 Music student Lara Miller was published in the Encore Program Honour List for Musicology, the highest recognition in HSC Music.

The Oxley Otters, a cycling team made up of Oxley teachers, participated for the third time in MS Australia's Sydney to Wollongong Bike Ride.

Nearly 100 Oxley students participated in the Duke of Edinburgh Award Scheme, working towards achieving their goals in the skill service, physical activity and adventurous journey components.

In a few of the many sporting highlights achieved by Oxley's athletes and sports teams, in ISA Tennis, Oxley's Division 2 team won their championship match and in Football, the undefeated 16s were ISA Premiers in their competition. Zoe Binder won the U15s women's cross country in the National Mountain Bike Championships in Adelaide (she won it again in 2011) and at the Mt Buller Mountain Bike Festival, Peter McKellar Stewart (Year 12) was named Junior Champion, winning all three stages of the competition.

Left: Cross Country running
Above: The Cross Country Camel Trophy

The camel trophy was given to David Wright and Peter Craig by Jeff Spender. Of the trophy's origins Peter Craig said, 'The turf wicket had been maintained at the old De La Salle school after it had closed and before it became Oxley College. A team from Bowral captained by Jeff Spender played a visiting team from India in a friendly game on the ground and was presented with the camel as a memento. Jeff passed it on to our fledgling school and we decided to use it for the Cross Country trophy. Rather unique, don't you think?'

This page: Students and staff from KSG Apeldoorn during the Dutch school's fourth annual visit.

Lifelong friendships were forged during these exchange visits, which began in 2006, as part of the 400th anniversary celebrations of Dutch–Australian relations. In the months leading up to 2006, discussions took place in The Hague between the Australian and Dutch Governments. An Old Oxleyan who was working in the Australian Embassy suggested Oxley College as a host school for Dutch English language students. He phoned Peter Craig, who jumped at the opportunity, and so began a long, reciprocal association between the schools.

Above left: Duke of Edinburgh hike

Above: Combined Argentina and Oxley Cricket Teams

Left: Equestrian changed to a summer sport in 2010 due to the placement of events throughout the year. During a successful season Oxley was represented by 23 riders at six events.

2011

The College began the transition towards allowing all students to use their own devices (iPads or laptops) to support their learning – also known as BYOD.

In a few of the year's many sporting highlights, the undefeated Boys First's Basketball team won their ISA Grand Final, as did the Boys 13s Football team. For the first time in the history of the College, Oxley entered Hockey teams in each ISA age group division, with all five teams playing in their semi-finals. Max Moran (Year 9) played in the U17s Country Boys Cricket Squad and Harry Boyce was selected for the NSW Country Rugby team. Rebecca Wool (Year 12) was named Captain of the NSW Equestrian team at the National Interschool Equestrian event in Victoria and Edwina Hutton-Potts (Year 11) was sashed Reserve Champion Grand National Rider, 15–U17 years, at the Sydney International Equestrian Centre and her horse was sashed Top 10 Hack of the Year. William Orchard was awarded first place in the U19s Southern Division 90km cycling road race, and in Water Polo, Gabriel Standen, Daniel De Rosa and Joshua Lemon represented the ISA at the NSW CIS Water Polo Championships, coached by future Olympian Chris Dyson.

In Drama the Senior Production was two short plays *Fewer Emergencies* by Martin Crimp and *15 Minute Hamlet* by Tom Stoppard, staged together. The Junior Production was *The Government Inspector*, by Nikolai Gogol. In the Fast and Fresh Theatre Festival, Oxley received awards for Best Male Actor (Sebastian Bailey) and Best Play.

Year 10 students sat the last ever School Certificate examinations.

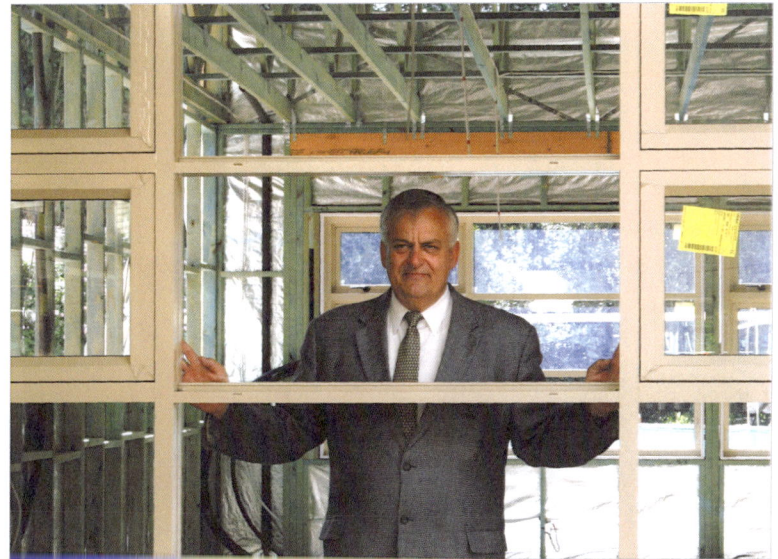

Above: In September foundations were laid for the new K–6 classrooms. As the concrete foundation of the new Oxley Junior School was being poured, Grant Williamson phoned Chris Welsh to tell him that the dream they shared was finally becoming a reality. Both men persisted in their efforts, over many years, to establish a Junior School at Oxley College.

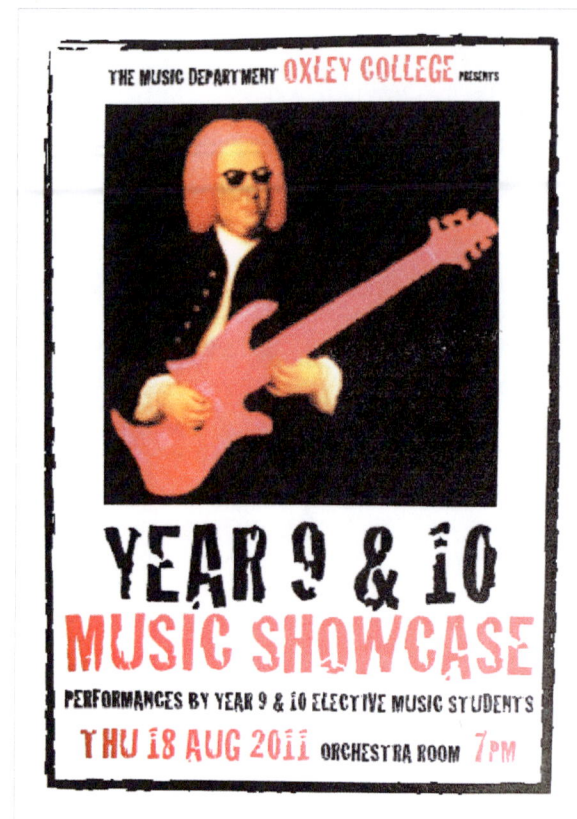

Left: The Oxley Otters, a staff team of cyclists who participated for the fourth consecutive year in the 'MS Gong Ride', from Sydney to Wollongong. (Left to right) Robert Hughes, Jan Ryan, Simon Woffenden (rear), Steven Armstrong (front), Danielle Carroll, Stuart Bollom (rear) and Steve Marnoch (front).

Above: Flyer for the Year 9–10 Music Showcase and (below) the cassette image featured on the program cover for the annual HSC Music Recital Evening.

On the Year 11 Outback Trip a new cooking trailer was trialled. Designed by Caitlin Guy (Year 12) for her Design and Technology HSC course, it surpassed all expectations.

The Oxley vegetable garden was established and Food Technology students entered a range of preserves in the Pavilion section of the Robertson and Moss Vale shows, with many receiving awards.

Oxley First XI Cricket Team participated in the Dream Cricket Day at Bradman Oval in Bowral. An initiative of the Movement Disorder Foundation, Rotary and Cricket New South Wales, the team acted as mentors and coaches for primary school children with special needs. Teacher Steve Marnoch reported that:

The Oxley cricketers all participated with great enthusiasm and found themselves immersed in the day, helping and playing games with children less fortunate than themselves. To a man, they found the day immensely rewarding as they made new friends, won the hearts of many young kids and even met and chatted with the Dream Cricket Day patron, former Prime Minister John Howard.

Artworks of Year 12 Visual Arts students Byron Kelly and Eleanor Lawless were selected for the ARTEXPRESS exhibition, featuring the best of HSC Art in New South Wales.

An after-school robotics workshop was introduced and master classes in nuclear physics were offered as part of the Enrichment Program.

Above: In 2010 Jasper Fearnley (Year 10) won the 'Life at Oxley College' Mural Design Competition, for a wall mural to be situated in the Outdoor Learning Area (OLA). A group of Year 9 students (Angus Ashbrook, Edward Capel, Jordan Grice, Bryson Masters, Toby Orchard, James Sutherland and Hugh Walker) painted the mural during September OLE week in 2011.

Initiated by Mr Williamson, the 'Life at Oxley College' mural had to include the five main virtue headings as outlined in Oxley's Strategic Directions 2009–2013. Of her design Jasper said:

'The mural depicts an image of the Pin Oak Tree, which is one of the symbols of Oxley College, representing strength, and is a microcosm of school life. The roots represent a deep grounding in the earth, knowledge and nurturing. The attributes indicating the Strategic Directions are interwoven within the design of the root system. The tree trunk and branches represent the support network at Oxley College and the leaves represent life's seasonal changes. The bright green young leaves move from spring life through to autumn's aging and withering leaves. The acorns represent new life (Oxley students) with each having the potential to grow to a great oak. The birds in the tree are our companions in life and also represent the spirit.'

Leadership is about taking responsibility and working hard to help others who are in your team, whether that team is a sports team, a music group, one of our Houses or part of the many activities we undertake at Oxley. Leadership is about service. Leadership is about helping others.

Grant Williamson, 'Heads Comment', Weekly Record, 4 November 2011

Oxley hosted exchange students from Germany, Peru and the fifth annual reciprocal visit by students from Dutch School KSG Apeldoorn. Oxley students and staff visited Apeldoorn during a tour to Holland and the battlefields of the Western Front. The group also travelled to Belgium, France and Turkey. Upon their return Peter Craig received the following message:

Recently I attended the 8pm service at the Menin Gate in Ieper, Belgium. A number of young people (aged about 15 years I guess) representing your school were there too. Three of them, proudly wearing their school uniforms and with great dignity, laid a wreath tribute to the WW1 fallen. I know very little about Oxley College but, as a fellow Australian, I was very proud of all these young Australians. If these kids are representative of all students at Oxley, then you and your staff are doing something very good indeed. I respectfully suggest that you don't change a thing because, whatever you are doing, it is working well. Congratulations to you and your staff, to your students and to their proud escorting teachers.

In other travels, Ancient History students, staff and parents enjoyed an incredible trip to Italy, visiting Rome, Naples, Capri, the Amalfi Coast and Florence.

Old Oxleyan Matt Perger (2008) won the National Barista Championship at the 2011 Australian Specialty Coffee Championships.

Edward Smith (Year 9) performed in the Premier State Ballet production 'Paquita' at the Riverside Theatre. It was his first professional ballet performance.

Top: Foundation Day Year 12 tree planting with Head Boy William Lawson and Head Girl Charlotte Blake with tree and shovel.

Above: Head of College Grant Williamson with Oxley Governors Richard Rowe, Frank Conroy AM (Chairman) and Professor Brian Farrow (Deputy Chair) who stepped down from the Board at the end of 2011.

Opposite: Rugby Coach Tristan Bevan and the First XV Rugby team. In 2011 rugby and hockey teams from Tristan's old school, Christ's Hospital, in Horsham, West Sussex, visited Oxley on a sports tour and played matches against Oxley. One of their players, Joe Launchbury, has since played rugby for England. Oxley players pictured include Will Sutherland, Harry Reid, Cameron Meaney, Nick Brennan, Gabe Standen and Assistant Coach Andrew Lawson.

Above: Holland and Battlefields tour, October 2011

Right: Orientation Day 2011

Opposite: A misty Equestrian Day morning at the Roche family property, Araluen

This page: Oxley Junior School Day 1

2012

Oxley Junior School opened with 140 students in classes from Kindergarten to Year 6. Steven Armstrong, formerly Deputy Head of the College, was the inaugural Head of K–6 Department. Grant Williamson acknowledged the significant effort made by many people to enable the first intake of students in 2012, thanking the Oxley College Governors for their confidence in the project and Mrs Harris and the executive team for the endless hours of planning and preparation.

In April, 58 students and five sports coaches travelled to New Zealand as part of the largest international tour undertaken by Oxley. Football, hockey, netball, tennis and rugby matches were played across the South Island and Wellington.

Over 100 students across Years 5–12 performed in *Grimm Tales*, directed by Phil Cunich and Chris Canute. Oxley entered the Impro Theatresports School Challenge for the first time.

Oxley debaters entered the HICES debating competition for the first time, with outstanding results.

Right: Junior School opening (left to right) Frank Conroy AM, Chairman of Oxley's Board of Governors, Pru Goward, Member of the New South Wales Parliament for Goulburn, Grant Williamson and Ken Halstead, Wingecarribee Shire Mayor.

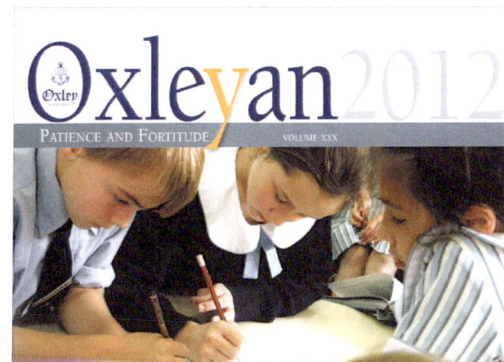

Above: Junior School students

Right: 2012 Year 12 Farewell Tunnel

… always remember to live life to the fullest, take each and every day by the scruff of the neck and do everything you possibly can — try drama, public speaking, wildlife safaris, stamp collecting, camel racing, goanna pulling, whatever's out there — throw yourself at it and give it a crack. By doing this you'll find out what life is all about and what your true passions in life really are.

Sasha Mielczarek, Old Oxleyan, Foundation Day Speech 2012

Students in Years 9 and 10 travelled to Vietnam and Laos on a World Challenge tour.

Among highlights in Art, Year 12 students visited artist Ben Quilty's studio and four students had their HSC work nominated or accepted into the ARTEXPRESS exhibition.

Stewart Falk was one of 76 students Australia-wide to receive a Future Leader Indigenous Award for 2012.

Oxley hosted Dutch students and staff from KSG Apeldoorn for the sixth year. Four French and two German exchange students also attended Oxley and their host students enjoyed a reciprocal exchange later in the year.

Top: Althletics Carnival

Above left: Farewell events were held to acknowledge the significant contributions of two long serving, highly valued staff members, Judy Deitz (left) and Trish Topp. Mrs Deitz retired after 29 years teaching Food Technology at Oxley and Mrs Topp left Oxley after a distinguished career as a teacher of History and Studies of Religion.

Above right: Junior School French students and teachers celebrating La Fete Nationale (Bastille Day)

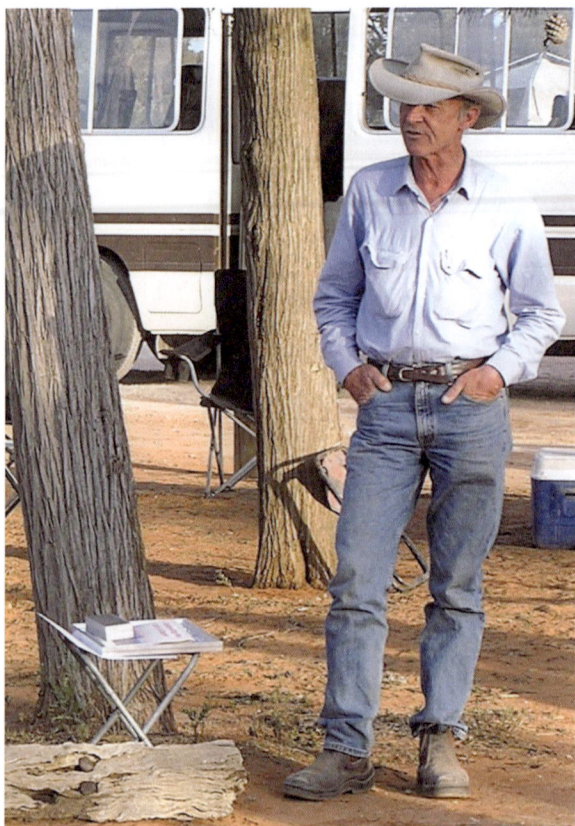

Helmut Schaefer

Vale, a dear gentleman whose knowledge and vision was boundless like the great Outback he revered and shared with so many, many people.

Peter Craig, 2012 Oxleyan

VALE

Helmut Rudolf Schaefer (1946–2012). A Memorial Service celebrating Helmut's significant contribution to the life of Oxley College was held on Sunday 26 August 2012. In a memorial published in the 2012 *Oxleyan*, Peter Craig wrote:

The Oxley College community lost one of its foundation pillars with the death of long-time staff member Helmut Schaefer. A consummate professional, Helmut was an old-fashioned schoolmaster who gave hours of his time well beyond the norm to generations of Oxley students. He joined the staff in 1986 to teach languages, both German and French, but his influence spread far beyond the Language Department which he led for many years.

... For many past Oxley students Helmut's name is synonymous with the annual (and now traditional) Year 11 Outback Trip. Proposed in 1988 by Helmut when the College sought projects to recognise the Bicentenary of the landing of the First Fleet, it was such a success that it has become a staple of life at Oxley. Hundreds of Year 11 students over the years have come back from a two-week camping trip that has taken them off the beaten track to such places as Willandra, Wilpena Pound, Oodnadatta, William's Creek, King's Creek Station, Uluru and Lake Mungo in awe of the Australian Outback. Stories of incidents on such trips are part of the fibre of the College and Helmut organised and developed the first 24 trips, a phenomenal and heroic effort.

As the Seniors Master at Oxley for many years, Helmut was involved in a wide range of activities. He ran leadership camps, held senior assemblies and took students to MUNA (Model United Nations Assembly) in Canberra. For several years, he raised money for, and took Oxley College students to East Timor, where he had established contact with the staff of two primary schools. He edited the school magazine and for years was the driving force in the College's Mock Trial team, which in 2005 reached the State Finals under his guidance. He was always willing to lend a hand, and one of his significant contributions was to assist in building the fleet of kayaks that Oxley students first used on the Wingecarribee River nearby. At times, Helmut joined the College's Executive as the Acting Assistant Deputy Head.

The Oxley College Alumni page on Facebook, which took over 4,500 hits (following his death), was awash with tributes from past students, staff and parents who wished to recognise the contribution that Helmut made to their schooling. The following encapsulates some of their feelings.

'Mr Schaefer embodied everything that was so fantastic about Oxley, and the experience he created in the Outback trip was a true coming of age moment. He will be sorely missed.'

'A true Renaissance man, I am thankful for his teaching and support during my time at Oxley.'

'My memories of Oxley and Outback are full of Mr Schaefer's ready smile and approachable nature.'

Above left: Georgia Matthews was awarded the prestigious Pierre Coubertin Award, which celebrates the Olympic spirit and the ideals of sport and sportsmanship.

Above right: James Slaughter holding the Oxley College Century Bat after his name was added for his century on 22 October against St Patrick's College. The perpetual trophy records the names and innings details of all players who score a century for the College.

As of 2023 the Oxley Century Bat has 59 separate plaques from 39 individual players. There are 14 players with more than one plaque and Robert Malcolm has four, the highest number of plaques belonging to one player. There is one double century recorded, achieved by Stephen McNaught, who scored 200 not out against Blue Mountains Grammar School on 5 December 2009.

Right: Oxley Day 1st XV Rugby

2013

A formal Gala Dinner was held in November to celebrate Oxley's 30th birthday. The evening raised $16,000 towards school sporting grounds.

A College master plan was developed to determine the additional buildings, sporting areas and other facilities that would be required in the coming years.

Year 12 Drama students performed at the annual Fast and Fresh Theatre Festival, where Oxley won awards for Best Play, Best Director, Best Actor (Luther Canute) and Best Actress (Samara Low). Michael Turczynski and Declan Moore were selected to perform in ONSTAGE.

Macquarie University Planetarium students presented an interactive lecture to students from Years 3–11. The night sky was projected onto the ceiling of a large inflatable dome and students lay on the floor to listen and learn about constellations, galaxies, the life cycle of stars and planets in our solar system.

Above right: The inaugural K–6 Equestrian Day was held at Shibumi Equestrian Centre near Bundanoon.

Opposite: Year 7 camp

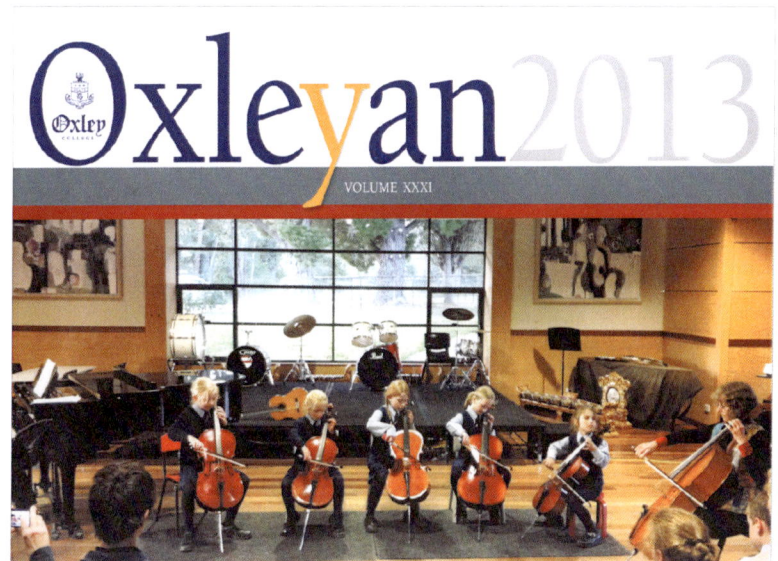

Oxleyan 2013
VOLUME XXXI

13s Football team

Playing together for the first time as a team, the boys had a most successful inaugural year of Football. In the 2013 *Oxleyan*, coach Stewart Forlonge said of the team: 'If the critieria for measuring the extent of achievement of a football team over a season are the level of enjoyment that the team members gain from playing, the degree of camaraderie that developed over the season, the extent of observable skill development and the collective positive attitude to training and playing, then 2013 can be considered a most triumphant season for the Oxley College 13s Football team.'

The inaugural Stephen Family Bursary was presented to the Year 11 Dux during Speech Night. The bursary was donated by descendants of Septimus Stephen, who built *Elvo* in the 1880s as a holiday residence for his family. Now known as the Stephen Family Award, it was donated by Martha Campbell, Caroline Parker, Mary Tanner, Sophie Wilson and William Rutledge. William is a grandson of Colin Stephen and presented the first award.

In team sports, a few of the year's many successes included Grand Final wins for the Girls Hockey Seconds, Netball Intermediate A Team and the Junior School Netball team. The 13s Boys Basketball team were undefeated premiers, as were the 1st XV Rugby Team, who had a record breaking season. Rugby coaches Brendan Fannin and Nicholas Combes said of the 1st XV Rugby captain, Michael Joubert, 'His leadership, management skills and tactical awareness were remarkable for such a young man and his individual playing skills were equally brilliant.'

In softball the stellar efforts of the Firsts Softball team and Junior A team saw Oxley named joint winner of the Softball Shield (with Chevalier) for the best performing school in the competition. As noted in the 2013 *Oxleyan*, coach Simon Woffenden said the Softball Firsts captain, Shalmali Yadwad, was: 'an inspirational leader of the team as well as an outstanding player ... She has led by her actions, words and attitude and has at all times been positive and encouraging.'

Charlie Dummer (Year 8) was selected for the U15 CIS NSW cricket team and Old Oxleyan Max Moran was selected for the ACT cricket team at the U19 National Championships in Hobart.

Drama productions Little Shop of Horrors *by Howard Ashman (scene pictured) and Shakespeare's comedy,* A Midsummer Night's Dream *were staged during the year.*

The Visible Learning teaching framework was introduced to Oxley College in 2013. This new approach was articulated by a shift in focus from being taught to learning. The Deputy Head Academic at the time, Kate Cunich, said of Visible Learning:

In 2012, when the Junior School was added to our existing Senior School, we looked to best educational practice to inform the K–12 learning journey. Professor John Hattie had just released his meta-analysis, Visible Learning, as a study of maximising impact in student learning. For this reason, Oxley's leadership team used the framework to develop a shared language of learning for students, teachers and families.

Harnessing student feedback and regularly joining students in the classes were part of a foundational practice that helped guide the learning journey. Teachers used learning intentions and success criteria to make progress and growth visible to the students, and students shared their strengths and challenges as they analysed their own learning and set learning targets.

Oxley's journey was recorded as a chapter in 'Visible Learning in Action: International Case Studies of Impact'. Staff continue to be invited to help other schools, with some having the opportunity to present at International Educational Conferences to share our experience as an early adopter of this powerful educational framework. Most importantly, Oxley's students speak the language of learning as they develop the deep understandings that will take them through their lives as lifelong learners.

This page: Inaugural Junior School House Poetry competition participants and winners

Oxley College is a K–12 school that utilises Visible Learning to make a difference for our students. This learning extends well beyond the set subjects and we need to be constantly aware of the minds we are shaping and the responsibility we have to encourage our students to think.

Grant Williamson, Head's Speech, Speech Night 2013

Left: Oxley Day produce for sale. Below: Fast and Fresh Drama Festival rehearsal

In Visual Arts the HSC works of students Tiffany Allen, Zuni Garcia Clarkson and Georgia Matthews were selected for ARTEXPRESS.

Rearrangement and curation of the David Wright library. This included the creation of two separate non-fiction sections for senior and junior collections. Books identified to be retired were sent to schools in Papua New Guinea while books of historic value were archived.

A vegetable garden and 'chook palace' was built by volunteer students, parents and teachers Ms Brochard and Mr Woffenden.

A new staff study area was opened for Year 7–12 staff.

Left: 30 Year Gala Dinner Committee, Tina Allen, Orissia Turczynski, Fiona Nixon, Veronica Kennedy-Good and Jacqui Pugh.

Below: Junior School Christmas carols

Recognising the importance of roundness and balance in young people, Oxley believes that learning extends beyond the classroom. The broad program of activities offered at Oxley is designed to provide further opportunities for students to discover themselves and to test their personal resources.

Frank Conroy AM, Chairman's Address, Speech Night 2013

Thank you and farewell

Steven Armstrong resigned after 27 Years teaching at Oxley to begin a new adventure at Trinity Anglican College in Albury. Steve said he had done every job at the school apart from groundsman. He began as a Mathematics teacher in the school's fourth year, when it had just 120 students in Years 7–12. During his last two years he ran the Junior School. Steve saw massive changes throughout his years at Oxley, from chalkboards to interactive smartboards, the addition of K–6, calculators and more. In an article published in the Southern Highlands News and the 2013 *Oxleyan*, Steve said of his years at Oxley:

> 'My early memories of the school are of the camaraderie between parents, students and staff. I taught my four-unit maths class in the garden shed. It was originally a chapel but we turned it into a garden shed. It was a big leap. The school was new and every week exciting – we came up with new policies every week. … I used to go to the secretary in the early days and we were only allowed one piece of white chalk a day.'

Steve taught a second generation of students at Oxley and said he had literally taught whole families. 'It's about learning about the relationship with the student, not the subject. I've enjoyed every moment in the classroom. There isn't a day where I haven't learnt something from a student.'

Steve Armstrong with Junior School students

MICHAEL PARKER

Headmaster of Oxley College 2014–2018

Michael Parker was born in Sydney and educated at North Rocks Public School and James Ruse Agricultural College. After completing school he attended the University of Sydney, where he obtained Bachelor of Arts and Laws degrees, as well as a Diploma and Masters of Education.

Michael moved to the Southern Highlands with his wife Fiona and their daughters Julia and Eleni prior to commencing at Oxley in April 2014. His previous school appointments include three periods at Cranbrook School in Sydney, interspersed with a year exchange teaching English at Eton College in the UK, and a period as Head of English at Newington College in Sydney. At Cranbrook School between 2007 and 2014 Michael's roles were Head of the Senior School and Deputy Headmaster. During this time he wrote three professional publications, including two editions of the book *Talk With Your Kids: Conversations about Ethics and Big Ideas*.

Prior to his appointment at Oxley College, Michael authored several legal studies textbooks as well as a student book and teacher's guide to teaching philosophy to children. With his wife, Dr Fiona Morrison, he co-authored a best-selling textbook, *Master in Pieces*, published by Cambridge University Press, Melbourne in 2007. Endowed with an abundance of creative energy, Michael's key recreational pursuit is writing creative fiction for children and adults.

In consultation with the Oxley Board of Governors and Staff, Michael significantly transformed and rebranded Oxley, creating a new vision and mission. Academic performance improved as new teachers were attracted and retained. The number of students attending the College increased rapidly, creating waiting lists in some years for the first time. These achievements contributed to higher parent, student and staff satisfaction and a strong relationship with the Board.

Key liberal academic changes Michael introduced or expanded across Years K–12, with assistance from Head of Academic Learning at Oxley, Kate Cunich, were the *Visible Learning* program, focusing on 'enlightened academic rigour' and a Year 12 study centre and program. Michael created, wrote and taught all the lesson plans for a new subject, *Cornerstone*, a core Year 7–10 course in big ideas, ethics and philosophy. Other new subjects introduced during his tenure were *Academic Writing; Global Perspectives*, for Years 9–10; the *Big History* course in Year 9, a whole school mindfulness programme and *Wide Reading* for Years 7–10. The popular Rites of Passage programme for Year 9 was created and overseas trips to one of Oxley's partner schools in Nepal, Botswana or Fiji were introduced for cultural and social service.

Michael has been active in many co-curricular educational spheres both locally and overseas. Sport became compulsory for Years 7–12 during his tenure and Oxley achieved the highest participation rate in the ISA (Independent Schools Association) of 95%. ISA competition gradings improved, particularly in Rugby.

Michael and the College Building Committee realised several building projects, including the design and construction of a new classroom block; the development of unique learning spaces throughout the College including the Year 12 Study Centre; the conversion of the canteen into a cafeteria; construction of tennis courts with new Score Board for the ovals; expansion of the K–6 campus; and the creation of three football and hockey fields in 2018. Under his watch the Oxley alumni was re-established and an Oxley Archives programme was begun, with the assistance of long term staff member Joanne Richards and former Governor, Linda Emery.

Michael's interests include reading fiction (including the Booker Prize shortlist each year) trekking and traveling. He has undertaken four major treks in Nepal, climbed Mt Everest past Camp One on the Tibetan side, been on 10 nine day wilderness (Outward Bound) camps in Australia and went ice climbing in Scotland.

Independently or with his family, Michael has made more than seventeen trips to Nepal, India, Tibet, Sri Lanka, Vietnam, Laos, Cambodia, Hong Kong, Indonesia, East Timor, Morocco, Botswana, Syria, Lebanon, Jordan, USA and most countries in Europe.

Michael and his family were farewelled by Oxley College at the completion of the 2018 school year, following Michael's resignation to take up the position of Headmaster at Newington College in Sydney.

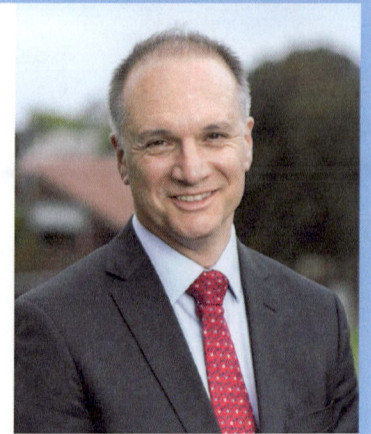

2014

Grant Williamson completed a seven year term as Head of College at the end of Term 1 and Michael Parker commenced as the new Headmaster in Term 2. At his first speech night Michael Parker reflected:

I have loved getting to know this very, very good school over the last eight months. Most of the students are remarkably friendly, open and adroit. I was told there was a vibe in the air and there certainly is. This is manifested in the frank enthusiasm and work ethic of many of the classes I have taught this year, the cheerful openness during recess and lunchtime or the extraordinary spiritedness of some of the House events such as the Drama House night and the talent competition just 24 hours ago. Indeed at that event people read poetry, played classical music, our Head Girl and Year 11 Dux did a fully costumed belly dance and the staff rock band, including four vocalists, did a brilliant rendition of Bon Jovi's 'Living on a Prayer'.

Launch of new Oxley College Vision and Mission: the heart, mind and soul of Oxley College. Michael Parker said of the process, 'In 2014 we created—or recreated— a vision and a mission that reached back into the past... indeed the past of the founders and of David Wright, to set course for the future. That vision was for Oxley to be a place whose combination of enlightened academic rigour, care for the whole child and cultural richness in a Southern Highlands setting makes for an education that is not surpassed in New South Wales.

A 'Headmaster List' was created to recognise outstanding academic effort and the teaching of philosophy was introduced for years K–6. 'Would you rather your child was smart or good?' was a hypothetical question Michael Parker was known to ask.

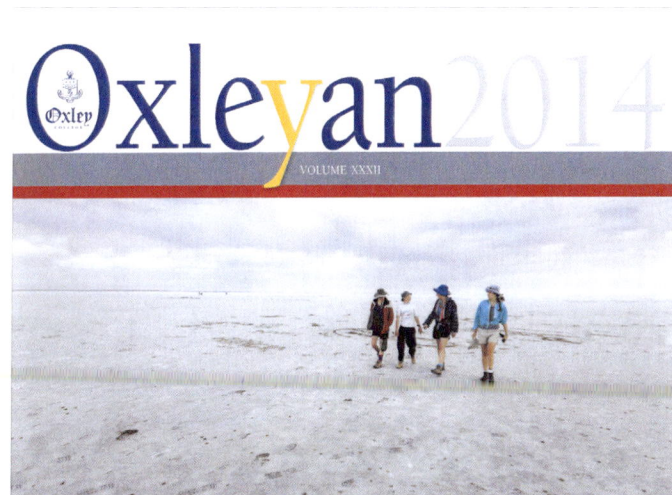

We are at an inflection point in history; a new decade, a new century, and nearly one and a half percent into a new millennium. The last time that sentence could be said was the year 1014 during the dark ages in Europe where Vikings ruled the sea.

Henry Bradley, Old Oxleyan's speech, Foundation Day 2014

Michael Parker with students and Jasper Fearney's mural in background (left), and serving in the Canteen (above).

The first issue of Pin Oak was published on 25 July. A fortnightly newsletter produced by a student editorial team and staff members Beattie Lanser and Emma Calver (Head of Marketing and Public Relations). *Pin Oak* replaced the *Weekly Record* newsletter which was published from 2010 to 2013. Students across all year groups were encouraged to contribute copy for reviews, opinion pieces and feature articles to *Pin Oak*. The writing has been fresh, informative, polished and at times, controversial. The inaugural co-editors were Ruben Seaton and Annabel Santo. In his first 'Editor's Letter', Ruben wrote:

Let's begin with a statement. A good magazine is like a burger. A good magazine is juicy, it's stimulating, it's packed full of content. It has a meaty patty: the letter from the Head Chef Mr Parker, fried in the oily goodness of Mrs Cunich and Mr Ayling. A good magazine has crunchy lettuce and ripe tomatoes: the feature article and Big Issue article respectively, providing a healthy and worldly dose of nutrition. It has regular columns to provide some relish, and a side of chips: a K–6 page to keep the young'uns happy. Turn to the music page for some melted cheesy jokes, or to the back page if you want the final touch: sports, with some caramelised onion if you so desire. All held together by the wholegrain, whole-hearted Ms Lanser bread and sprinkled with the greatest herbs and spices (student contributors) in Australia. And so, we are proud to present the first ever Pin Oak Burger: more than enough to dig your teeth into.

Year 10 students were offered the opportunity to accelerate their HSC studies in Legal Studies and Chemistry, enabling them to complete these subjects in Year 11.

MAGAZINE

PIN OAK

ISSUE 01: Term 3, July 25 2014

Welcome to the first issue of the new Oxley College fortnightly magazine.

On the Branch   Sports News   K-6

Above: Girl on swing. During OLE week students painted murals in the style of the artist Banksy on the outside walls of the Art rooms. Using spray cans, students learnt about using stencils and layering tones to create special effects.

Left: Cover of Pin Oak Issue 1. The inaugural Pin Oak team comprised Ruben Seaton and Annabel Santo as editors, Grace Naughton and Heidi Bevan as photographers, designers Emma Croker, Conor Lynch, Grace Naughton and Ruben Seaton, and staff editors Beattie Lanser and Emma Calver.

JUMPING CASTLE

SAUSAGE SIZZLE

FACE PAINTING

ZOO

CRAZY HAIR

HOUSE OF HORROR!

FLOOR HOCKEY

ART EXPRESS YOURSELF PEOPLES CHOICE AWARD ★

OXLEY FAMILY DAY

BUSKERS BUSKERS

OXLEY GARDEN PRODUCE

SUNDAY 10 AUGUST 10:30AM TO 2:30PM

BIG HAM BURGERS

DRESS UPS

Junior School Book Week, students in costumes (above left), and staff in Dr Seuss hats (above).

Far left: Oxley Family Day. Oxley Day initially began as a day where most Year 7–12 Oxley sporting teams had a home game on the same Saturday. The ISA competition grew to a point where it was no longer possible to provide schools with a Saturday of home games, so the P&F created the Oxley Family Day, filled with activities for the whole family, from Years K–12.

Left: Students with Oxley vegetable garden harvest.

Long serving staff members Max Ingall and Peter Craig retired. The foundation Deputy Headmaster at Oxley, Peter shared his vast knowledge of history with Oxley students for an incredible 31 years. He coached sport, founded the Oxley Alumni Association, organised international programs and was described as 'an Oxley institution'* and 'Oxley's own living encyclopedia'†. He was the last original staff member to retire and the Peter Craig Centre is named in honour of his long association with the College.

Max Ingall taught geography for 24 years, was Head of Florey House for 18 years and coached basketball and rugby. When Max started at Oxley there were 273 students, no computers or photocopiers and about three telephones. He remembers lining up with other teachers to receive his allocation of a stick of chalk each day from the Bursar.

Student exchange between Oxley and Dutch school KSG Apeldoorn. Oxley students also visited the Netherlands, the Australian battlefields of the Western Front and Gallipoli, Paris and Istanbul as part of a History and Art excursion.

The 'Bring your own device' (BYOD) policy was implemented.

'Wide Reading' and 'Booked Up', library programs were launched for students in Years 3–10 to encourage reading and The Gibraltar Club was introduced, where students engaged in university style tutorials.

Top: Max Ingall and Peter Craig

Above: During the 2014 Holland and Battlefields Tour, students placed a wreath at the Last Post Ceremony held nightly at the Menin Gate in Ypres, West Flanders, Belgium. A tribute to British and Commonwealth soldiers who died defending Ypres during WWI, the daily ceremony began in 1928.

* Frank Conroy described Peter Craig as '...an institution at this College' in his Chairman's Speech, Speech Night, 2014. *Oxleyan* 2014, p.27.

† Old Oxleyan Harry Bradley described Peter Craig as '... Oxley's own living encyclopedia' in his 2014 Foundation Day speech. *Oxleyan* 2014, p.25.

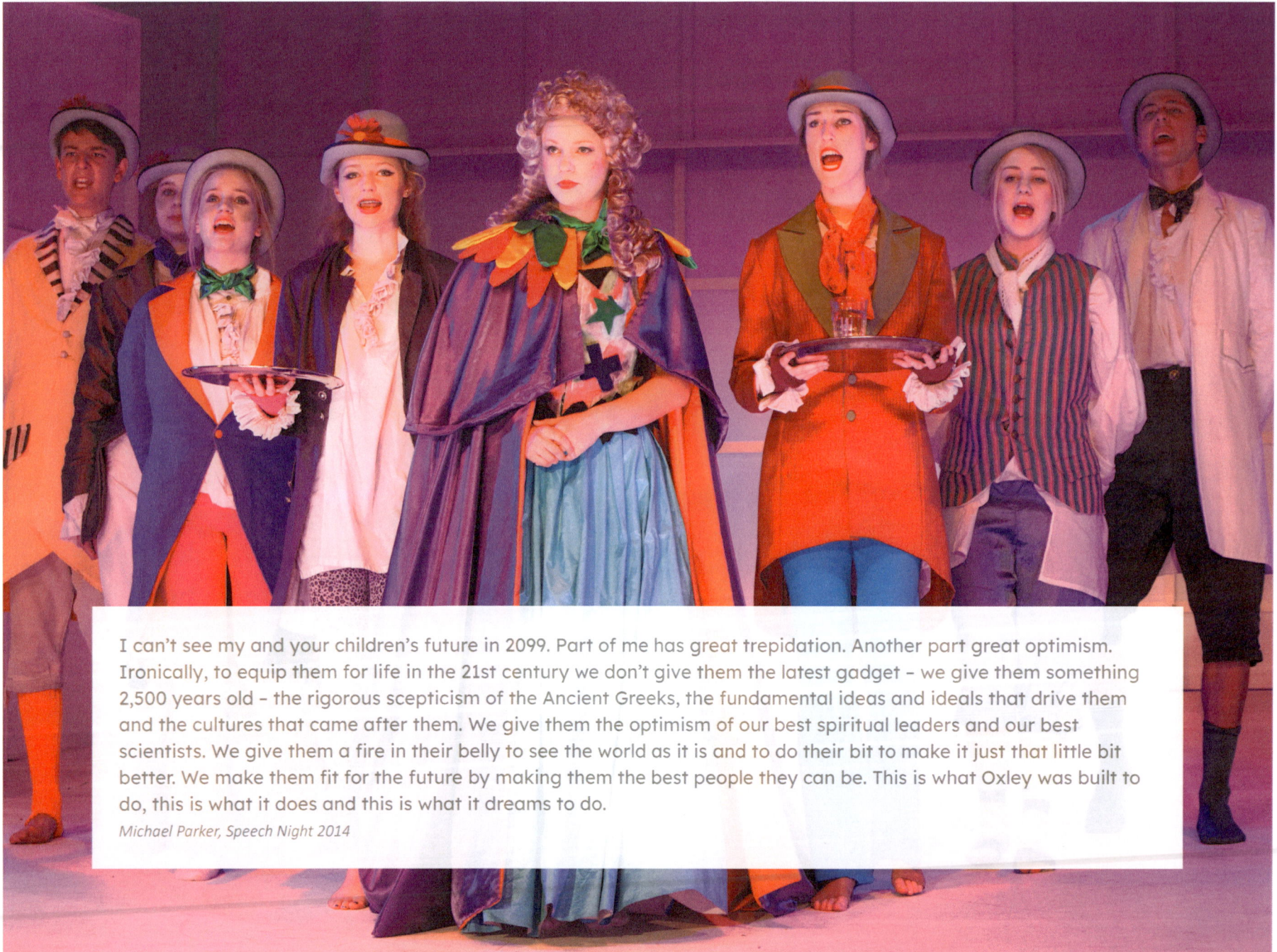

I can't see my and your children's future in 2099. Part of me has great trepidation. Another part great optimism. Ironically, to equip them for life in the 21st century we don't give them the latest gadget – we give them something 2,500 years old – the rigorous scepticism of the Ancient Greeks, the fundamental ideas and ideals that drive them and the cultures that came after them. We give them the optimism of our best spiritual leaders and our best scientists. We give them a fire in their belly to see the world as it is and to do their bit to make it just that little bit better. We make them fit for the future by making them the best people they can be. This is what Oxley was built to do, this is what it does and this is what it dreams to do.

Michael Parker, Speech Night 2014

A memorial garden between the Peter Craig Centre and The Pavilion was created in memory of Roxanne Spreag, a Year 11 student who was killed in a tragic traffic accident on Norfolk Island, where she lived. In 2022 a memorial seat was donated to Oxley in her memory.

The Oxley Garden stall, an initiative to share and sell eggs and produce from the vegetable gardens, was held on the main oval. Food Technology students made and sold food and drink and the funds raised were put towards garden maintenance.

The Senior Drama production was *The Wonderful World of Dissocia*, by Anthony Neilson and the Junior production was *The Visit*, by Friedrich Durrenmatt.

Year 12 Visual Arts students Zoe Binder and Lachlan Wild had their HSC major works selected for ARTEXPRESS and Head Girl Evangeline Larsen (Year 12) was named Oxley Poet of the Year.

Junior School students raised funds for Korovou Village School in Fiji, to help provide a library and new school roof.

Among the year's numerous sporting achievements, Harry Kooros was selected for the 2015 JML Sydney mountain bike racing team, Georgia Wade and Harry Norman (Year 9) were awarded Hockey scholarships through the Illawarra Academy of Sport, Sacha Kroopin (Year 7) was named Junior Ladies 10-metre Air Pistol State Champion and 25-metre Sports Pistol Reserve Champion, and Harry Jensen represented Oxley at the NSW All Schools CHS PSSA Cross Country Championships.

Tristan Bevan taking a photo of students on Outback (photo by Michael Pugh)

JUSTINE LIND

Head of the Oxley Junior School 2015 – 2019

Justine Lind commenced at Oxley in 2015 in the third year of the life of the Junior School. She was appointed by the then Headmaster, Michael Parker, as the inaugural Head of Junior School. In his *Pin Oak* article to the community announcing her appointment, Mr Parker commented, 'She is already brimming with ideas to take the Oxley K-6 School into the next decade.'

Prior to joining the Oxley community, Justine worked in a number of Independent Schools as a teacher and leader of curriculum to transform the learning landscape for primary school children and their teachers. In 2014, she completed a Master of Educational Leadership at the University of New South Wales.

Passionate about the imperative to prepare all children to enter the Wisdom Era as compassionate and confident change-makers, Justine values innovative learning experiences that honour the innate capacity of young children and empowers them to appreciate their own unique preferences and talents.

During her time at Oxley, Justine and the extraordinary team of teachers with whom she had the privilege to work, re-envisioned the curriculum to deliver concept driven inquiry experiences that provided opportunities for challenge, choice, collaboration and creativity. This approach emerged out of her study into the Wisdom Era to identify the future focussed competencies that will be required in years to come. The evidence of best practice from the field of Gifted Education, aligned with this approach to elevate the engagement and relevance of the curriculum and to leverage the strengths of all learners. Learning Showcases, Student Portfolios and Student Led Conferences empowered students to be in the driving seat of their own learning and involved the wider community in a variety of celebrations of learning.

The nature of her contribution to the Junior School reflected her vision to create an inspiring learning community for students, teachers and parents. The evidence base of the educational approaches of Visible learning, Understanding by Design, Cultures of Thinking and Reggio Emilia, informed the approach to curriculum design and delivery as well as the physical learning environment and the documentation of the learning process.

The culture of welcome was enhanced through more formal weekly assemblies and additional community events such as Grandparents' and Grandfriends' Day. Student voice and agency was emboldened through the establishment of the Student Representative Council and Environmental Committee and our leadership development program integrated our own version of Peer Support through the Seat Project in 2018.

The Junior School established a place of wonder that honours the students through aesthetic beauty, art works, sculpture from Hillview and artist in residence projects as part of OLE Week each year. In 2019, the long-anticipated addition of the treehouse was completed to which one precise student commented was 'not a treehouse but a house next to a tree'.

Justine concluded her tenure at Oxley, under the leadership of Jenny Ethell who reflected on the quality of her leadership. 'Justine has led the Junior School through an exciting journey. She has transformed the learning landscape from its fledgling stage into the dynamic learning community of today. It is a place where students are empowered to engage deeply with significant ideas and complex issues and by doing so demonstrate their extraordinary capacity through their work, conversations and actions.'

As part of the 10th Anniversary of the Junior School in 2022, Justine was delighted to be invited to contribute to the Foundation Day ceremony to celebrate this milestone. She reminded us that staff, students and families alike play a vital role in influencing and sustaining the values and character that make Oxley such a distinctive and much adored place in the lives of so many.

2015

During the year many of the 7–12 classrooms were rejuvenated and restyled into exciting and innovative learning spaces, with the installation of themed photographic wall murals. Rooms included:

The Himalayan Room: Prayer flags and statues from several different cultures complement a majestic image of Mt Everest.

The Trinity College Room: Parquetry floor and a Persian rug lead to a trompe loeil image of the Long Room at Trinity College in Dublin. The visual effect is one of standing on a balcony overlooking the whole library.

The Green Room: Featuring a serene image of a Japanese garden across the complete back wall, floor to ceiling.

The Bioshock Room: The mural image in this room initially appears to be a Great Gatsby Party in space, but it is actually an underwater scene, from a computer game called Bioshock.

The New York Room: With its board table, leather chairs, clocks in four time zones and a wall sized image of the New York skyline, Business Studies students feel more like they are running the world than learning about it.

The French room was restyled as a Parisian Cafe and the Mathematics classroom included a gallery of eight foot high Escher artworks, and a mural of Einstein with his equations turning into stars in the sky.

Michael Parker said of the refurbishment, 'These rooms didn't come from a 'Class Murals R Us' style website or company. We had to create these from the ground up and we don't know of any other schools in NSW (or on the planet) who have anything similar. We feel that they make a strong and significant difference to the learning environment.*

Justine Lind, Head of Junior School

*Michael Parker, Headmaster's Report, *Pin Oak* Issue 11, 2015, p.4.

Right: New York City Skyline room
Below: Japanese Garden room
Opposite: Himalaya room

Education is all about the future. It is about hope for our world and the audacious dreams of its people. Schools, however, must be lived in the present as they become a world of their own for the children who inhabit them.

Justine Lind, K–6 Information Book

One of the best moments of the year involved the Year 10 Cross Country championship where a new student to Oxley, who was winning, quite literally, by a country mile, was misdirected in the last 400 metres and ended up doing two laps of the oval instead of one. Another boy crossed the finishing line first. He took the winner's baton over to the first boy, dropped it at his feet and said 'I think this is yours'. This is the Oxley spirit, where honour and integrity are more important than winning for the sake of it. We had two winners that afternoon.

... Earlier this year I got to see the way the Academic side works from a student's eye perspective. Ben Canute won a students' competition to have a senior teacher go to all of their classes, do all their work for them and do all of their homework. The senior teacher was me. On the morning, we swapped ties and books, but he didn't give me his school lunch. He also didn't tell me that the very first period was – a Maths test. I desperately studied circle geometry outside the classroom from his book for the one minute before we went into class and did the test. In the periods in between I went to fascinating Design and Technology and Science lessons. In the last period, Music, we were studying the structure of rock songs and we had to finish the one we were doing for homework. Ben put up his hand and said 'Miss, I am really interested in this subject, could I please have extra homework'. Which I then had to do.

However, on a serious note, spending the whole day AS a student was fascinating. I saw the rich variety of methods teachers used, I saw the depth of some of the ideas, I saw how technology was used, I saw how discussion was used. I learnt more doing that than in a week of external Professional Development workshops.

... When we at Oxley teach critical thinking, rationality, creativity, respect for others' opinions, love and empathy, we are deliberate about growing flowers of steel. We might be in Bowral, not London or Paris – and thank God we are – but we are carefully, deliberately cultivating the citizens of the future to live in a world that is complex, multilayered and needs to be protected from the fundamentalist forces of utter black and white. We will continue to do that.

Extracts from Michael Parker's Speech Night address, 2015

The Year 12 Study Centre opened on the top floor of *Elvo*. John Rapp, a member of the Board of Governors and Head of the Board's Building Subcommittee, steered and oversaw the entire Study Centre building program. Year 12 students can be found studying in the Centre from 7am to 7pm where they are supported by a Year 12 Academic Master.

Cornerstone was introduced as a new subject for students in Years 7–10. Devised and written entirely at Oxley, Cornerstone is based on discussions, hypotheticals and open-ended questions, drawing together big, inspirational and ethical ideas.

Implementation of Mind Matters (and Kids Matter for the Junior School) a program designed to support and improve mental health, resilience and well-being.

Inaugural Year 9 'Rites of Passage' experience. Students enjoyed an immersive three weeks in Sydney visiting museums, art galleries, universities, climbing the Sydney Harbour Bridge, camping on Cockatoo Island, attending performances at the Sydney Opera House, and more. They even went on television asking questions on Q+A. Oxley teacher and convenor of the trip, Bronwyn Tregenza, said of the program, 'We offered Year 9 the chance to travel, look and learn in Sydney to broaden their horizons and education. City children will visit the bush to learn country skills – we take our country kids and let them learn in the city.'*

Above and opposite: Gold Duke of Edinburgh students on a hike

*'Rites of Passage for Oxley Year 9', *Southern Highlands News*, 22 July 2015, p.26.

OXLEY COLLEGE
engaging, enriching, extending each child

7-12
Information
2015

Oxley

The Oxley Bagpipers was formed, under the guidance of tutor Rob Parker. The first step to becoming a bagpiper is learning to play the chanter. Drumming students also began their lessons.

Oxley opened its Instagram account. There are now two official Oxley Instagram accounts – @oxleycollege, and a student led page – @t.h.e.o.c.

Drama Productions were *Out of Order* by Ray Cooney and *Telling Wilde Tales*, by Jules Tasca. The K–6 Drama production was *Out of this World*.

Establishment of a charitable initiative and relationship with a village in Kathmandu, Nepal, entailed fundraising for projects, overseas service trips where Oxley students teach at the local Primary and High Schools, and post HSC 'gap year' visits.

Year 10 created a 'Ball Pit' where students who didn't know each other could slide into the pit and ask each other searing questions from a laminated list. Questions such as: 'What are three things on your bucket list?', 'Have you ever been shocked by an electric fence?' and 'Would you rather be a genius in a world of morons or a moron in a world of geniuses?'

Top right: Oxley's contribution to the Empire Art Walk. In commemoration of the 100 year anniversary of the Bowral Empire Cinema, students of local Wingecarribbee High Schools were invited by Miel and Gerry Kroon to create art works for the walkway beside the cinema.

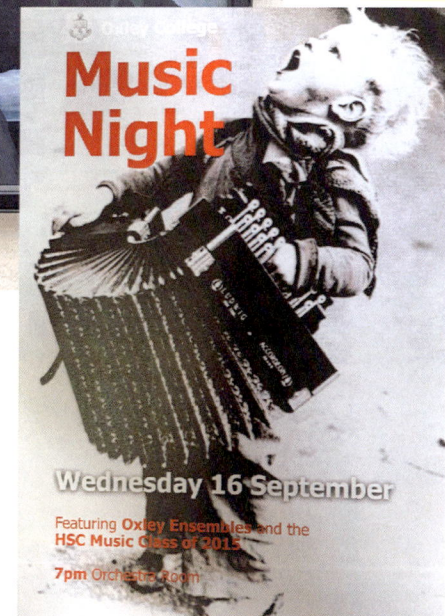

OXLEY COLLEGE

Music Night

Wednesday 16 September

Featuring **Oxley Ensembles** and the **HSC Music Class of 2015**

7pm Orchestra Room

Students in Years 5, 6 and 10 took part in the Oxley College 'Sleep Out', an overnight fundraiser for Father Chris Riley's 'Youth off the streets'. Bedding down for the night in 'difficult conditions' the sleep out raised over $2,200. Coordinator Isabella Davies (Year 10) said of the experience:

… students now have a greater understanding of the number of young people affected by homelessness and some idea of what they experience each night.*

* 'Oxley sleep out for street youth', *Southern Highlands News*, 4 November 2015.

Creation of ELVO Acknowledgement Register – a record for students and teachers to record acts of kindness. The inaugural entry recognised Year 1 student Thomas Bladen for helping a fellow classmate to finish a cross country race by saying, 'Come on Aislinn, we can share our energy, let´s run together!'

Classroom 'Walkthroughs' were introduced to gather data about student learning.

Amelia Worthington (Year 12) achieved first place in Mathematics General 2 in the HSC.

Year 12 Mandarin language student, Hugh Dawkins, spent two weeks in Ghanzou, China with 150 other students from around the world, on a trip sponsored by the Chinese Government.

Cricket matches between Oxley College and combined schools from Jaipur, India were held at Centennial Park, supported by Cricket Australia. Oxley cricketers also visited the United Kingdom for a three-week cricket tour.

Sascha Kroopin (Year 8) won the National Pistol Championships in Adelaide, becoming the 12–25 year group Ladies 10m Air Pistol National Champion and Equestrians Rosie Bowyer, Hunter Taylor, Will Quirico and Amelia O´Sullivan competed in the Australian Interschool Championships at the Sydney International Equestrian Centre.

VALE

A much loved Year 7 student, Angelique Burton Ho, tragically passed away during the year. The Angelique Burton Ho Award for courage and tenacity in a Year 6 student was created in her honour and it was awarded for the first time on Speech Day 2015. In his address that evening, Michael Parker said:

I have seen Oxley as a place of great courage and resilience this year. After the tragic loss of Angel Burton Ho in Year 7 all of the students grieved together and supported each other in those terrible days of hearing the news and attending the funeral. They made heartfelt speeches, sang songs and raised collections. She absolutely loved her life at Oxley. She played hard despite her challenges and quirky ways and won the hearts of all those she met. Angelique will always be a part of Oxley College and never be forgotten.

2016

Moments of academic life observed by Deputy Head of Learning Kate Cunich, during the year included, 'Year 10 Cornerstone students in groups on *Elvo* lawn, earnestly discussing (in peer-led discourse) and grappling with the big ideas of the interrelationship of art and beauty, wisdom and age, dreams and regret, life and death. Year 8 History students in Medieval costumes (with Nike shoes underneath), being shown weapons and jousting, feasting on fine food, learning by doing in the glorious grounds, accompanied by a student playing harp.'*

A K–6 Student Representative Council was created.

A group of Year 7 girls, led by Zoe Brain and Julia Parker, formed the Gorilla Girlz. During World Environment Week they aimed to collect 1,000 preloved mobile phones, iPads, computers, iPods, MP3 players and their chargers for recycling. Money raised was donated to 'Gorilla Doctors' in support of efforts to save critically endangered gorillas.

The inaugural Oxley Year 10 Film Festival was a highlight of Term 3. Organised by Ms Cox, groups of students created and produced a short film, with help and guidance from a dedicated team of teachers and film industry professionals. The completed films were premiered at the Empire Cinema in Bowral, complete with red carpet and paparazzi. Student Jordan Colby described the popular event as 'An experience of a lifetime'.

Pin Oak Issue 30

Year 8 Medieval Feast: Student musician Thomas Tregenza entertaining Year 8 Medieval Feasters (above left); Knight in shining armour (above right).

Opposite: Year 10 Film Festival: the paparazzi

Global Perspectives was introduced as a new subject for students in Years 9 and 10. A stimulating, cross curricular and skills-based course built around a series of topics, each of global importance, the course encourages the development of critical thinking and teamwork.

Social service trips were undertaken by Year 9 students to Oxley's sister schools Sedie Middle School in Botswana, Jib Jhibe School in Nepal, and Village School, Korovou in Fiji. The Oxley community donated $10,000 to Jib Jhibe Village to assist with rebuilding their secondary school, which was badly damaged in an earthquake. The donation also funded an internet connection for the remote mountain school and paid a teacher's salary in the primary school for a year (the equivalent of about $500).

Romy Healy (Year 10) visited the village of Mbita, in Kenya, Africa with her father and friends to build houses for widows and their children and other service work. Money raised during Oxley's annual Mission Day helped improve the lives of an entire village. In the words of Romy, 'Oxley has done a tremendous thing and it has had a very real impact.'

Exchange students from KSG Apeldoorn, a school in the Netherlands, visited Oxley for a week. Organised by Mr Tim Dibdin, the trip marked the 10th anniversary of Oxley's partnership with KSG Apeldoorn.

Opposite: Year 9 students in Nepal, with teacher Christophe Gauchat

Top: Sienna Knowles and Lucie Drysdale in Nepal

Above: Tully Mahr (Year 9) in Korovou, Fiji

Left: Volleyball in Nepal

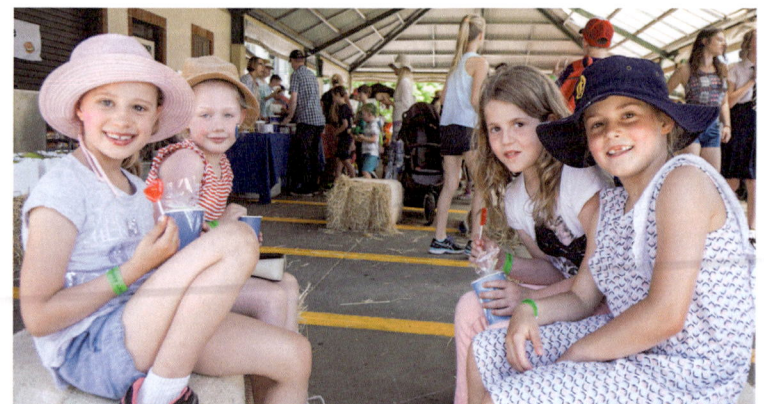

Inaugural Pin Oak Fair was held on November 12. Under the banner of 'The Spirit of Giving' the College was transformed into a country fair of old, with rides, races, sport, market stalls and an art exhibition titled 'Emerge'.

Roslyn Hamilton, Head of the Languages Department and Senior French Teacher at Oxley, retired after 18 years at Oxley and a career in education spanning 40 years. Mme Hamilton said her years at Oxley were her happiest. In a farewell tribute published in *Pin Oak* Issue 42, Michael Parker wrote,

'... when she arrived here, after 10 years at a big Sydney private school, it was as if she had gone to educational heaven. Teachers were able to teach with a smile, to actively engage in the learning of students instead of wasting precious learning minutes on discipline. Students meet the eyes of adults, smile, and even offer to help! Manners are remembered and there is friendship and joy to be present at Oxley.

'... she had several French students in the top 10 in NSW in the HSC and several students have added their ability to speak French to their talents (a diplomat, a winemaker in France, an international lawyer, a pilot are examples). A devoted hockey coach she twice won the Open B ISA Hockey Competition in her 15 years of service to the sport. There was also a 'development year' in which no goals at all were scored! She says her success was in teaching the girls to fake graciousness that year. She will not miss the early morning starts for the hockey bus but she will miss greatly her students and colleagues.'

Jamie Pryor was selected to participate in the 21st National Schools Constitutional Convention, held at the Museum of Australian Democracy in Canberra.

Above: Elvo the poet tree
Left: Mme Roslyn Hamilton
Opposite: The inaugural Pin Oak Fair

There were many memorable moments in the sporting arena, a few of which follow. Gabby Taylor Helme played in the NSWCIS Netball 'Team of the year' who won the All Schools Challenge, and Charlie Dummer (Year 11) played in the NSW City Country Schools Cricket team, competing at the State Championships. Kiara Rochaix (Year 10) was selected for the NSW All Schools U19 and Australian U19 Football teams and was a member of the successful NSW All Schools Girls Football team. Oxley hockey stars Jamie Binder, Cate Patterson, Kaarina Allen, Catriona Uliana and Georgia Wade made up 50% of the ISA Hockey team who competed at the NSWCIS tournament and budding Hockeyroo, Georgie Wade (Year 11), was scouted for the prestigious NSR programme that promotes athletes to universities throughout North America.

Oscar Moran played head prop in the NSW Country U16 Rugby Team that toured New Zealand, and Oxley Rugby 13s and 16s teams were named ISA Premiers, the 13s being undefeated all season. Cedric Hely (Year 11) received a Berrima District Sportsman Award for outstanding achievements in javelin and hurdles at the NSW All Schools Carnival, and Nicholas Milner scored a hat trick playing for the Oxley 14s cricket team against East Bowral cricket club. Oliver Deakin (Year 4) played in the unbeatable Moss Vale Magic U12 Basketball team, who were named Southern Junior League Champions.

Oxley Equestrian team members Hunter Taylor (Year 8), Anneliese Wansey (Year 7) and William Quirico, were selected to represent NSW at the National Interschool event, achieving high results in the five day competition, and Oxley Softball had a successful season, jointly winning the Champion Softball School shield with Chevalier. Oxley's Softball Captain, Cate Patterson, played in the winning ISA team at the NSW CIS Softball Championships, the first time in 23 years the team had won the competition.

Above: Year 12 Drama students (2015) in an Onstage performance directed by Phil Cunich, at the Seymour Centre in Sydney in February.

Opposite: The Senior Drama production Pippin was staged in Hoskins Hall during March.

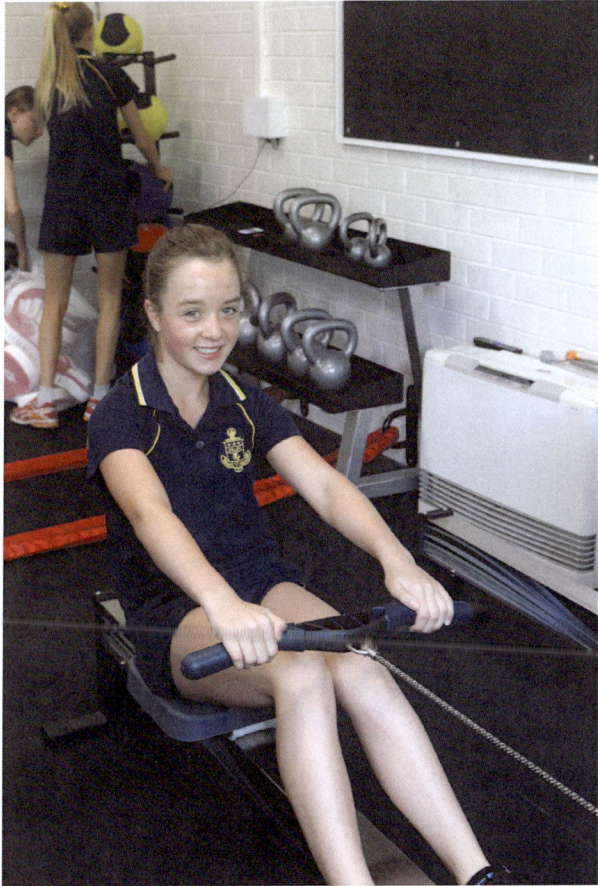

Above: A new fitness facility was opened in the Peter Craig Centre, with early opening hours and professional instructors from The Shed gym in Bowral on hand.

Exercising in the morning sets up the rest of your day, giving you more energy and a feel good attitude.
(Tully Mahr, Year 9, Pin Oak Issue 41)

Opposite: Students on Year 9 Rites of Passage

Above: Year 11 Outback trip; Sophie Capel (right)

2017

Opening of a new, state of the art building with nine new classrooms.

The Creek Bed Project was initiated by the SRC to clean out the pond in front of the music rooms and introduce more native plants to complement those already growing in the wetland area. Liam O'Connell (Year 7) helped the SRC's vision come to life by planning the logistics of the project. He put forward a planting plan and organised the costs of rebuilding. With the help of the maintenance staff and a few keen students to undertake a working bee, Liam's idea was put into place and a thriving wetland garden exists today.

2017 was a busy year in sport for the Junior School. Oxley K–6 Athletics won the HICES Athletics Percentage Trophy. The Junior Hockey team won the Southern Highlands Hockey Association U11 competition and the inaugural K–6 Rugby match against Blue Mountains Grammar was played. In the 7–12 ISA winter sport finals Oxley won the Bs Hockey and in Snow Sports Chilli Sparke won gold in the Girls Individual Cross Country Skiing Championships, qualifying for the Nationals. Ravi Wikramanayake (Year 10) was presented with the Oxley College Centurions bat for the second time and Hunter Taylor represented New South Wales at the Equestrian Australia National Horse and Rider Competition.

Sophia Hamblin (Year 5) won the annual National History Challenge, a research based student competition, for her report on the Sydney 2000 Olympics.

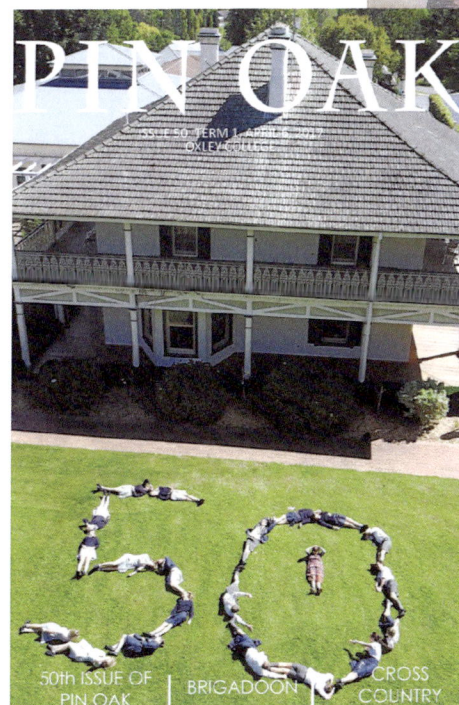

Top: Article from Southern Highlands News:

Student contribution for 50 years. *Pin Oak* editorial students Izzy, Harry, Imogen, Gracie, Jemimah and Jade at a lunchtime meeting.

Above: Cover of the 50th Issue of Pin Oak
Opposite: Staff photo

Above: Junior production, Phantom Tollbooth Jr
Right: Senior Drama production, The Book of Everything
Opposite: Ikea was performed across New South Wales

Senior Drama production – *Stories In The Dark* and *The Book of Everything*; Junior production – *Phantom Tollbooth Jr*, based on a book of the same name by Norton Juster. Two groups of Oxley HSC Drama students were nominated for the state *Onstage* production. One play, titled *Ikea*, performed by Ella Moran, Tom Hill, Sophie Capel, Mitchell Latham and Ryan Muir, was performed across New South Wales.

Founding principal Dr David Wright returned to Oxley to present his new book, *The End of Schooling*.

This page: 'Eve on the Green' was a highlight of the year – with over 1,400 tickets it was a total sell out and a wonderful success.

Oxley Canteen Manager Catherine Fraser with Geoff Jantz (top), made sure everyone was well fed.

'Eve on the Green', held on 25 November, was a highlight of the year and a huge fundraising success, with a bumper sell out show of over 1,400 tickets. The work of the Parents and Friends team, led by Bec Biddle, Kristie Phelan and Shelley Davis, was supported on the day by many volunteers from within the school community. It was a wonderful event and a memorable and joyful afternoon. John Waters and Leo Sayer led a host of performers from Oxley, Chevalier College and the Southern Highlands Christian schools in a fantastic showcase of young local talent on a massive mobile stage on the College green, while Geoff Jansz cooked up a storm with an army of parent volunteers. The event raised money to support our local BDCU Children's Foundation and their Youth Mental Health Initiatives, and for Oxley's sister school charities in Nepal, Botswana and Fiji.

This page: Michael Parker implemented an evening technology GREY OUT, suggesting an 8pm social media curfew for students in Years 4 to 9. Here the Heinrich family (below) show how it's done.

During Speech Night, Michael Parker reflected on the future and asked us to consider what it may look like. Extracts from his speech follow:

What will AI, climate, tech, resource scarcity and endless innovation do for and to us in the lifetimes of our children? How do we as the educational custodians of these people who will live their whole adult lives in the future discharge our responsibility? How do we make them fit for the future?

We have to do two things as a school. Firstly, we have to look forwards ... to immersing them in new technologies, ways of doing things and ways of thinking – be it creative innovation as a core competency, working flexibly in whole new industries, having the restless pluck and vim to throw everything out and start again, and having them think of themselves as citizens not just of our country but of this whole globe that's hanging there in space.

But here's the other thing – we also have to look back to what is core in our culture. Look back past any particular body of knowledge – which can now be conjured up in your hand by Google in a moment regardless – to critical thinking and to logic. To what is a fact and an opinion, what are the types of opinions, what are generalisations, to what's a truth and what's a lie. It is this astute juggling of the grandly old and the excitingly new that will help make these young people fit for the future.

It is a bit of hackneyed phrase that the future needs the 4Cs: Communication, Collaboration, Creative thinking and Critical thinking. I am going to add a fifth. I think the future needs, more than ever, Community.

If this is true, then one of the most important things we have as we head into the future is each other. Not virtual communities that are about as friendly as a warehouse full of shop mannequins, but real communities of real people travelling with each other through this life. Our society has fewer and fewer of these communities – guides, churches, sports teams. Which means that in our society probably the most important communities remaining for many people are schools – us.

Top and above: Book week

Top right: The first Oxley Fencing Championships were held in 2017

Right: Staff member Meaghan Stanton won the Masters 3 Women's race at the Cross Country Mountain Bike National Championships in Queensland, qualifying to compete in the Masters Mountain Bike World Championships in Andorra, where she placed 5th. As of May 2023, Meaghan has won 14 National Championship titles since 2017.

During the October holidays two thirds of Year 9 students travelled overseas for a cultural and service immersion experience at partner schools – Sedie Middle School, Botswana, Jib Jhibe School in Nepal, and Village School in Fiji.

VALE

Harriet Janet Elizabeth Nixon (1995–2016)

On Friday 6 January 2017, in excess of 1,200 people gathered in the Peter Craig Centre to honour Harriet, a much loved former student of Oxley College who lost her life following a tragic accident. Harriet's service was led by former Oxley Head Rev. Chris Welsh, together with Mr Charlie Scudamore, Vice Principal of Geelong Grammar School, Harriet's uncle, Father Plunkett OAM and Mr Dennis Mudd OAM – friend, former Principal of Moss Vale Primary School and Oxley College Governor.

Harriet represented Oxley both academically and in co-curricular activities including the SRC, hockey, music, Duke of Edinburgh, cross country, equestrian and community service. Harriet will be forever remembered for her love, loyalty and kindness to her friends and family – Ralph, Fiona and sister Alicia (a former Oxleyan), for her generosity of spirit, her beautiful soul and for the significant contributions she made to her life and to the many communities of which she was a valued member.

Fiona and Harriet Nixon at an Oxley Equestrian Day

There has always been a lot of kindness and generosity between the past Heads of College. They all had different messages, but they all have the same core values.

Emma Calver, Oxley Registrar

2018

Many special events were held during 2018 to celebrate Oxley's 35th birthday. At a number of these celebrations all the Heads of College, from the inception of the school, were together. Reflecting on these occasions during Speech Night, Michael Parker said, '... the arc of the College is long and what makes Oxley special is deep in its soil and consistent from its very earliest days until now and for decades into the future.' Towards the end of 2018 Michael Parker resigned to become Headmaster at Newington College in Sydney. During his final Speech Night he reflected:

> Oxley is a special place. For we are a beautiful, bucolic and vibrant place to spend your childhood and teenage years. We are small enough for each child to be known and large enough to give each child all the opportunities they need. We are young enough to be innovative and old enough to be steady. We are full of intellectual curiosity and we are full of care. We know exactly what we are about and I think we are wise beyond our years. I would like to thank you all for being such a wonderful, kind, interesting group of people whom I have enjoyed knowing and will miss. I often say that when you are kind Oxley is kind, and I saw plenty of examples of this.

> ... Another special feature of my year has been my Year 7 Cornerstone class with its usual mix of dead keen, reasonably motivated and completely disinterested students. The book marking, exam setting, report writing and so on keeps me connected. It was wonderful to have all the high level conversations about current affairs, Ancient Greek philosophy and the meaning of life. It's also good to have the edifying effect of having a group of kids see me as a class teacher first and a Head of School second.

Above: Founding Head of Oxley College Dr David Wright with Junior School students following the Foundation Day Special Oxley Head's Assembly.

Opposite: Foundation Day guests at the Special Oxley Head's Assembly, (left to right) Anni Baillieu, Roderick McAllery, Professor Brian Farrow, Peter Bray, Christopher Welsh, Dr David Wright, Olivia Donovan, Harrison Baillieu, Grant Williamson, Michael Parker, Linda Emery, Amanda Lawson and Frank Conroy AM.

Above: Past, present and future Heads of College at Oxley's 35th birthday dinner dance 'Made in 1983', held at the school. Left to right: Christopher Welsh, Dr David Wright, Michael Parker, Grant Williamson and Jenny Ethell. Michael (dressed as Nick Rhodes from Duran Duran) said he was the only one not to get the memo that costumes were not required for Heads!

Right: Parents and staff at at the 'Made in 1983' dinner dance.

Building projects completed this year included the Junior School climbing frame, the tennis courts and a remodelling of the area near the canteen, now known as The Pavilion. Solar panels were installed, the Parents and Friends Association contributed significantly to a new scoreboard on Governors Field and bore water was struck on Bray Fields, where work was in progress to have the playing surfaces ready for the next winter sport season.

During Oxley's first NAIDOC week assembly, members of the local Aboriginal community, including Aunty Trish, spoke to students and held a smoke cleansing and ochre ceremony. Gundungurra man Bodhi Matthews spoke about the history of the Gundungurra people, whose land the College stands on. 'The History and culture of the Aboriginal people is the history and culture of all Australians, no matter of ethnicity', he said and encouraged the school community to reflect on the history of the land and to learn more about the traditions and stories of the Southern Highlands.

Oxley's theme for NAIDOC week, 'Because of her, we can!', referenced Oodgeroo, also known as Kath Walker, after whom an Oxley House is named. In a speech titled 'Who is Oodgeroo?', Julia Parker said, 'I think 'because of her' we can see: see the suffering of the Indigenous people; see the importance of her home, people and land; see her passion for the education of Aboriginal children; see her longing for the conservation of land and culture. Also, I think 'because of her' we can talk. I hope that, on the long mission to understand each other's cultures, we will remember women like Oodgeroo, who showed us the power of dialogue. Her poetry invites us to talk to each other, to have a cultural dialogue.*

*Reflections of our NAIDOC week Assembly 2018, *Pin Oak* Issue 75, p.8.

Above: Pin Oak *Issue 64, showing off the new Junior School climbing frame*

Above right: *Long term staff members Kate Cunich and Emma Calver in The Pavilion*

Right: *NAIDOC week activities included an ochre ceremony*

Left: Lachlan Sell; Top: Ayla Cassar and Jesse Noad

Above: Euan Barrett-Lennard, Oxley's first Mountain Bike Captain, rocking the Oxley cycling kit.

Strong communities are not a fluke. They do not just 'happen'. They require respect for each other. They require effort. They require each member to think beyond themselves and their own needs. They require each of us to show care and consideration.

Grant Williamson, Oxley 35th Birthday, Special Head's Assembly

Cross Country Mountain Biking was introduced as a school sport. The program was started by Meaghan Stanton and Peter Dowse, who has managed many Australian Mountain Bike teams at World Championships, Commonwealth and Olympic Games. More than 100 students have taken part so far.

Kayaking was reintroduced as a sport, with 18 students participating under the instruction of former Oxley teacher and founder of Kayaking at Oxley, Ian Royds, a Level 3 Advanced Whitewater Instructor. The program ended in 2020.

Oxley students continued to perform at the highest level in sporting competitions, winning awards in ISA Cricket, Hockey, Softball and Netball. The Junior U11 Football team won the Michael Sant Cup. There were many outstanding individual sporting achievements. To mention a few Kiara Rochaix was selected into the Australian U19 Schoolgirls Football team touring America, Hugh Callaghan represented Australia in Youth Futsal (indoor soccer), touring Spain and Hunter Taylor was awarded Reserve Champion in the Equestrian National Championships.

Oxley uniform introduced long pants for girls in winter. A Driza-bone coat became a uniform option in 2019.

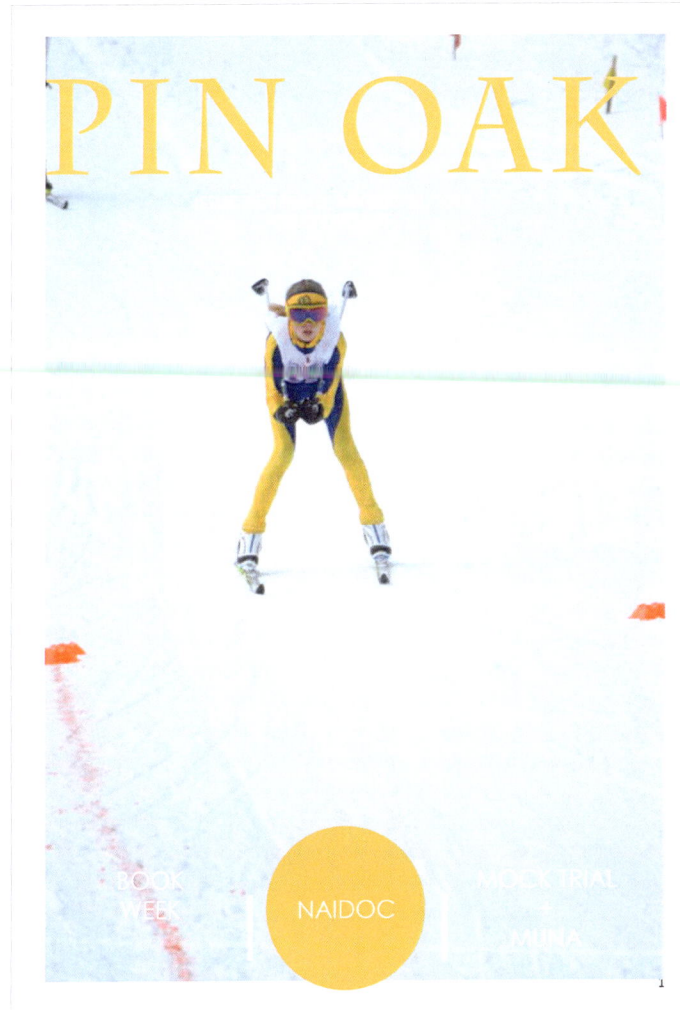

PIN OAK

NAIDOC

Snow Sport Champion Chilli Sparke (Year 6) on the cover of Pin Oak Issue 75

The Senior Drama productions were *The 25th Annual Putnam County Spelling Bee*, a musical comedy by William Fin, and the surreal *Where in the World is Frank Sparrow?*, by Australian playwright Angela Betzien. Both plays received Canberra Area Theatre (CAT) awards, including Best School Production and Ensemble for Spelling Bee and Best School Director, for Phil Cunich.

In other Drama news, Year 11 and 12 Drama students toured to New York and Melbourne and a theatre script written by Jemima Taylor (Year 11) was chosen to be professionally produced by the Young Playwrights Project. To complete a particularly exciting and successful year, Oxley's 2018 HSC Drama students were chosen to perform in the ONSTAGE production at the Seymour Centre in Sydney.

Above: Scene from Where in the World is Frank Sparrow?
Left and opposite: Scenes from The 25th Annual Putnam County Spelling Bee

My prayer for Oxley is that it will always be a school where every student matters. Where the values, the principles by which they live will be paramount. That a quality of heart will be wealth here that will help keep our whole nation generous and prosperous. It is the values that you and I cherish that will count for the most in the end.

David Wright, Oxley 35th Birthday, Special Heads Assembly

This page: The Oxley Pipe Band, performing at Brigadoon in Bundanoon (left) and leading the 2018 Bowral Anzac Day March (top).

Great coffee became available at Oxley with the opening of 'Off the Shelf', a coffee and hot chocolate dispensary accessible via the French courtyard near *Elvo*. The brainchild of Peter Ayling, 'Off the Shelf' sold coffee to students in Years 11 and 12 students and hot chocolate to those in Years 7–10. Year 9 students completing their service component for the Duke of Edinburgh were trained as baristas by Baeden Terry of Rush Coffee (Rush also provided the coffee beans). All the money raised from sales was distributed to Oxley's three partner schools in Botswana, Nepal and Fiji.

Two teachers from Sedie Middle School in Botswana, one of Oxley's partner schools, attended Oxley for three weeks.

D'Arcy Deitz (Year 12) was listed in ENCORE's honour list for HSC Musicology and flautist Lucie Drysdale (Year 12) was awarded 'The Associate in Music, Australia Diploma'(AMusA). Highly respected in the national and international music community, the Diploma is awarded by examination to outstanding candidates and recognises a sophistication of musical understanding and performance.

The Murray Walker Art Prize for a Year 12 work to hang in *Elvo* reception for five years was awarded for the first time at the 2018 Speech Night. Bodhi Matthews and Sascha Binder were the inaugural recipients.

Year 8 participate in Project Rockit, Australia's first youth designed platform aimed at developing empathy and leadership and providing strategies to address bullying.

Southern
Highland News
THE HOME OF SIR DONALD BRADMAN

$1.60

TOP RESULTS: Oxley College students Gabriel Kolovos, Juliette Swain, Jessica Deakin, Olivia Donovan, Caitlyn Jowett and Zack Cunich achieved strong results. **Photo: Supplied**

Our top achievers

Top: Year 12 Design and Technology student Jessica Deakin with her evening dress made out of upcycled plastic bags, which was featured in the SHAPE 2018 exhibition at the Powerhouse Museum in Sydney.

SHAPE showcases a selection of outstanding major works from the HSC Design and Technology, Industrial Technology and Textiles and Design courses. Many works by Oxley students have been included in SHAPE and ARTEXPRESS exhibitions over the years.

Above: 2018 Year 12 students on the front page of the Southern Highlands News *following the announcement of their HSC results. Gabriel Kolovos, Juliette Swain, Jessica Deakin, Olivia Donovan, Caitlyn Jowett and Zach Cunich.*

This page: In response to the drought affecting areas of New South Wales, staff member David Spies organised for students in Years 9 and 10 to visit the town of Murrurundi to assist with drought relief. Assisted by Jane Dummer, Simon Woffenden and Sue Hanrahan, students took a trailer load of donated groceries, along with supplies for a sausage sizzle to Murrurundi Public School. They also worked as volunteers on several properties, learning a bit about the realities of life on the land.

> **"**

Kathryn Cunich made a farewell address to Michael Parker on Speech Night. Extracts follow:

Late last term, we gathered in this place to listen to the three previous Headmasters of Oxley – Dr David Wright, Mr Chris Welsh and Mr Grant Williamson. Each had been invited by Mr Parker as part of the celebration of the school's 35th birthday. Each Headmaster told a story about what leading Oxley was like in their time, how much they relished their work at this great school and what the values of Oxley meant to them. The fact they came back on that day was not only a sign of respect to the past, but of the present and the future – speaking to the community of Oxley that is so special to many of us. So today marks the next time of reflection on Headship, starting formally for Mr Parker, as he packs up his things, his many, many books and begins to leave us, Oxley, behind, forever, not forgotten, but forever changed for his presence and leadership.

… Mr Parker has been our Einstein, challenging what is possible, turning the mundane into magic, leading us through glorious days at Oxley. When we first heard that Mr Parker was to be the new Headmaster, we all did what everyone does – googled him! And the first link: an SBS documentary featuring Mr Parker as an inspiring teacher. And that said it all, for us as staff, it was so important to know that we had a leader who had walked our path, who loved teaching, who loved children, who loved books, who cared for students and most of all, at this time in Oxley's history, thought outside the box.

The introduction of Cornerstone brought the opportunity for many of us to see Mr Parker in action, sitting in a circle, leaning in, smiling, engaged and inspiring, throwing in a big question (or three) or contemplation, discussing it in a way that all in the room had a voice. Michael has brought that approach to all his dealings with students, teachers, staff and parents. He is a people person, personable, approachable, humorous and sometimes accidentally doing very, very funny things. The staff will each have their own special memory of a moment when Michael made them smile. For example, our Monday morning staff briefings often had a very humorous moment to them as Mr Parker

thanked and acknowledged the hard work of the previous week, at the same time laying out what was ahead, invariably adding a story or anecdote that made us giggle and feel re-inspired for the week ahead.

The staff have been provided an easy bridge to speak to Michael, with Michael meeting regularly with them in the Common Room to hear any concerns and then address them promptly. Michael endorsed the formation of a Staff Wellbeing Committee, provided gym facilities, the most amazing coffee machine, introduced mindfulness and many other things for us. His sense of humanity, in understanding where staff were, are and will be has been commendable. Mostly though, we thank Mr Parker for embedding a vision and passion for student learning at Oxley, not just in the classroom but in the very bones of our curricular, pastoral and co-curricular programs, with quirks. Under his leadership we have a distinctive curriculum second to none, enriched by Rites of Passage, the Year 10 Film Festival, social service trips and a myriad of other stunning opportunities.

In 2014 Mr Parker announced that "We are bringing the heart of the school, to the heart of the school". We held our breath – Year 12, he was talking about you – the Study Centre at the top of *Elvo* was Mr Parker's way of giving you the sanctum that was needed for rigorous study, recognising how important it was to strive, stretch and stick. At the same time, he gave the staff a state-of-the-art staff study, complete with lounges, places to relax, pods to work in, changing rooms for sport, a hub of professional collaboration and planning.

Michael has stood beside sport coaches and students as they boarded buses on Saturday mornings, flown to Botswana to teach, been dunked at the Pin Oak Fair, dressed up in various costumes that made us laugh, inspired many of our students to become teachers by insisting that on a social service trip to Nepal, Botswana

and Fiji you don't just paint fences – you give back by making the biggest difference – by teaching little ones.

His model of rights and responsibility, for us as educators and students as learners, will long stand as a powerful symbol of the scales of balance required in education leadership at the moment – how we get it right in tricky times.

> … Dauntless in the face of challenge, always keeping the high goal in view … Great leaders leave many words, memories and visible signs of their leadership, not only on buildings, but in the hearts and lives of many people.

So for us, we are sad, sad to lose a visionary leader, one who truly has taken us on journey that has been 'Dauntless in the face of challenge, always keeping the high goal in view', striding in the pioneer's footprints, literally. But just as Dr Wright, Mr Welsh and Mr Williamson's words, deeds and actions are embedded into the very fibre of Oxley, so will be the actions and words and vision of Mr Parker. Great leaders leave many words, memories and visible signs of their leadership, not only on buildings, but in the hearts and lives of many people.

Michael, you have done this for us – a generation of Kindergarten to Year 12 students, families and staff, influenced forever. Oxley is a kinder place for your work: for when you were kind, Oxley is kind. To Fiona, Julia and Elena – we wish you well in your next chapter of life in Sydney with your husband and dad. Remember us … and like the words of our school song – always be brave and bold and true.

> **"**

JENNY ETHELL

Head of Oxley College 2019–2022

Jenny Ethell commenced as the sixth Head at Oxley College in January 2019. Previously, Jenny was Principal of Perth College – a leading independent girls' boarding school in Western Australia.

Jenny was educated at Curtin University in Perth where she graduated with a Bachelor of Business (Agric.) degree and a Graduate Diploma in Education. She has taught and occupied senior leadership positions at government, independent and catholic schools in Queensland, Victoria, Tasmania and Western Australia. Appointed as Principal in her 30s, Jenny was Principal of Perth College from 2003–2018 and Interim Principal at Methodist Ladies College in 2002. During her career Jenny has worked in single gender (boys and girls) and co-education settings.

Committed to life-long learning, Jenny has studied at Harvard University, the University of Melbourne and the Australian Institute of Company Directors. She has presented at and participated in a range of education conferences in Australia and overseas. Her longstanding experience and role as Principal has befitted the Association of Heads of Independent Schools Australia (AHISA) where she was Chair of AHISA's Western Australia branch and a Director of the National Board for a number of years. She also served on a range of educational bodies over recent years.

While some say Jenny's leadership at Oxley College has been marked with navigating the College community through unprecedented challenges, including drought, devastating bushfires, an ongoing global pandemic and some of the worst floods in living memory, it has been much more.

Throughout her time as the Head of College, Jenny made every decision with the best interests of the students at the centre, building trust in her leadership with the community. She oversaw considerable growth and change, bringing a mature model of leadership as the College approached its 40th birthday. Enrolments increased by more than 100 students and talented new staff were hired.

With the support of the College Board of Governors and Executive team, Jenny strengthened the culture of enlightened academic rigour amongst students and staff and brought clarity to the vision and core values of the College through the development of the Oxley Lens: Be Kind, Show Courage and Seek Wisdom.

With a vision to create a liberal education that is world class, Jenny continued to strengthen the academic offering and culture with the introduction of subjects like Environmental and Earth Science, Latin, Japanese, Personal Interest Projects and programs like Global Thinkers.

Visible impacts of Jenny's leadership were the transformation of several areas across the College including the house by the tree in the Junior School playground. With the support of the Building Committee, other projects included the refurbishment of the Library, Elvo and The Studio, Art, Design and Technology precinct.

Jenny is married to Dougall, former Chaplain of Hale School in Perth. They have four independent daughters who work in their chosen careers across Australia and the USA. Jenny and Douglas made the difficult decision to return to Western Australia during Term 1, 2022 to reunite with their family. Oxley College will always hold a special place in their lives.

I strongly believe the aim of education is to improve the human condition. Each person is unique and we all need to learn to know, learn to do and learn to live together.

Jenny Ethell, Head of College

2019

Jenny Ethell commenced as Head of College at the start of the year. In an interview with Year 10 student Ava Lambie for *Pin Oak* Issue 82, Mrs Ethell said:

The role of Head of College is to provide the vision and help develop the culture. It's like being an orchestra conductor. You have to get everything working in beat to make a beautiful sound.' Her advice to students included: 'Dream big. Dream about the world being a better place and dream about your place in the world. Work hard, because nothing comes without hard work and our world needs compassion and kindness, so be kind and caring and inclusive to others.'

A merit system recognising courage, humanity, justice and wisdom was introduced for students in Years 7–10.

The 'Act For Peace' Ration Challenge, inspired by Old Oxleyan and former Head Girl Karen McGrath (Class of 2007), took place during refugee week. During a fundraising 'Ration Challenge' organised by Year 12 students, sponsored participants in Years 10–12 ate only the same rations as a Syrian refugee received, for three or five days.

Oxley's environment group completed a waste audit of the school's rubbish disposal and made proposals to reduce landfill and increase recycling and reuse. Their strategies included composting, plastic free bins and encouraging nude-food days.

As part of the 'Solar Buddy Project', Year 10 geography students assembled solar lights which were delivered to children living in energy poverty in Papua New Guinea.

Above: Jenny Ethell with students

This page: Scenes from the Junior School production of A Kidsummer Night's Dream

The Senior Drama production was *The Crucible*, by Arthur Miller and the Junior School production was *A Kidsummer Night's Dream*. In the Short and Sharp play finals at the Parramatta Riverside Theatre, Tom Rapp was awarded Best Male Performance.

Oxley Pipe and Drum Bands performed in the pre-show program at The Royal Edinburgh Military Tattoo in Sydney.

PDHPE (personal development, health and physical education) syllabus was introduced in the Junior School and a new Technology syllabus was offered in Years 7 and 8. The curriculum included 3D Computer Aided Design (CAD), Computer Aided Manufacture (CAM) and coding.

The Parents and Friends Association donated nearly $30,000 to provide items for the school from a staff 'wish list', benefiting students from K–12. Items funded included water bubblers and the permanent courtyard umbrellas near the 'Off the Shelf' cafe. Among other activities, the Parents and Friends Association hosted a Christmas in July event at Burrawang School of Arts and continued to operate the Hungry Ox on weekend 'Home' sports days.

Cornerstone was extended to include Philosophy as a subject for Year 11 students.

The Oxley beanie was introduced as part of the school uniform.

Scene from The Crucible

Featured on the cover of Pin Oak Issue 92, and as part of 2019 NAIDOC week, artworks were created with Gamilaraay man Darren Dunn, based on the themes of Voice, Treaty and Truth. They are a reminder of important relationships and the journey towards greater understanding.

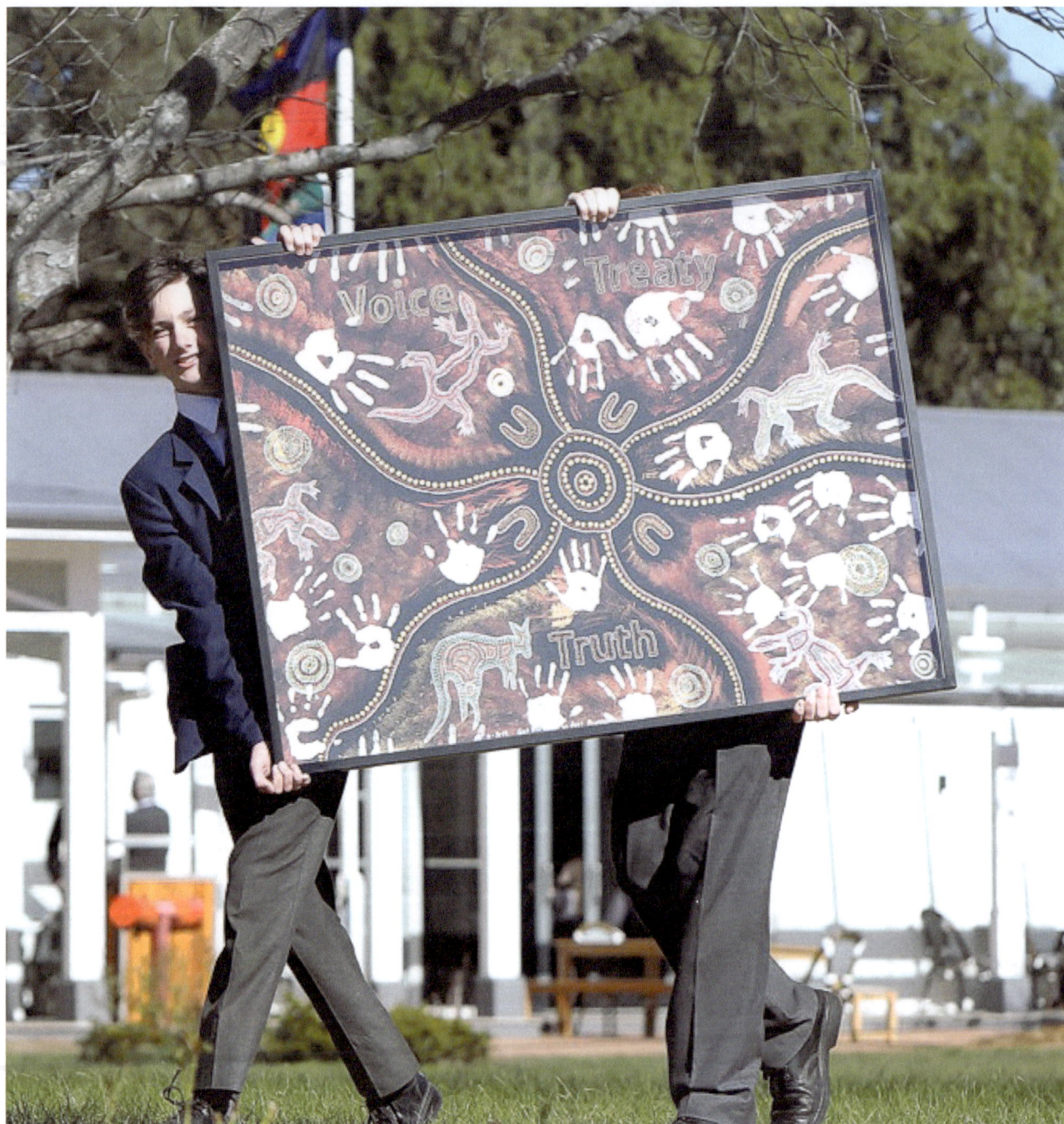

The Study and Supper Club was established for HSC students studying in the Senior Study Centre outside of school hours.

Justine Lind, Lara Sheils and Kathryn Cunich attended an international conference to present Oxley's pioneering work (in partnership with the University of Melbourne) in evidence-based teaching and learning practices. The inaugural Oxley professional learning conference was held, providing an opportunity for staff to share current and future research interests.

Year 9 debating students won Oxley's first debating trophy at the HICES.

In Oxley's OLE (Oxley Learning Experiences) program, students participated in a 120km mountain bike ride, went scuba diving in Jervis Bay, or travelled to Botswana, Nepal or Fiji to assist at Oxley's sister schools (students raised nearly $7,000 on Mission Day for these schools). Other students paddled 63km up the Hawkesbury River and the animal welfare group built possum boxes, wombat mange treatment containers and a koala enclosure.

In a few of the adventures undertaken by students outside the classroom, Madeleine Sargeant (Year 10) sailed as a crew member on a historic tall ship to Brisbane as part of the Young Endeavor Youth Scheme. Alison Brain (Year 11) represented Oxley at the Rotary Four Way Challenge, presenting a speech titled 'Learning on Country' and Skye Holmwood (Year 12) attended the International Youth Science Forum in Singapore.

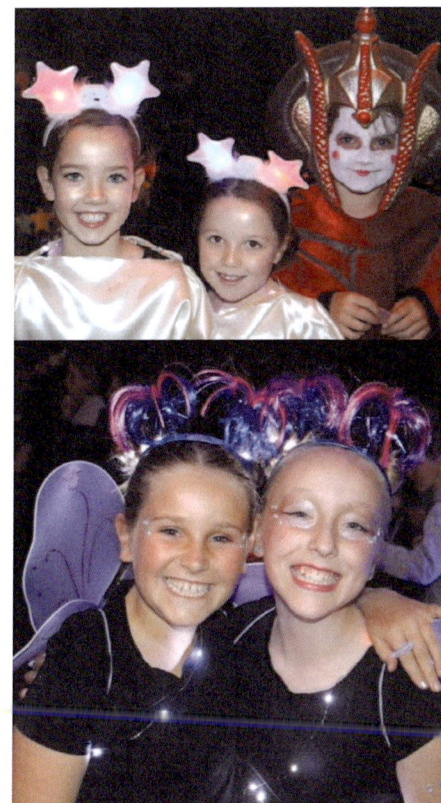

Left: Year 10 Film Night featured on the cover of Pin Oak *Issue 97.*

Above: The Junior School Disco

Above: Oxley Snow Sports team

Right: Pin Oak Issue 85. The Oxley Mountain Biking team participated in a number of categories in the NSW All Schools Championships and competed in The Willo marathon event in Wingello State Forest. In a field of over 500 riders Oxley had some standout performances. Euan Barrett-Lennard placed 3rd (U19 male) in the 44km race, Lucy Cavanough Quince came 2nd (U17 female) in the 22km race and placed 2nd overall, and Lachlan Blair placed 6th (U17 male).

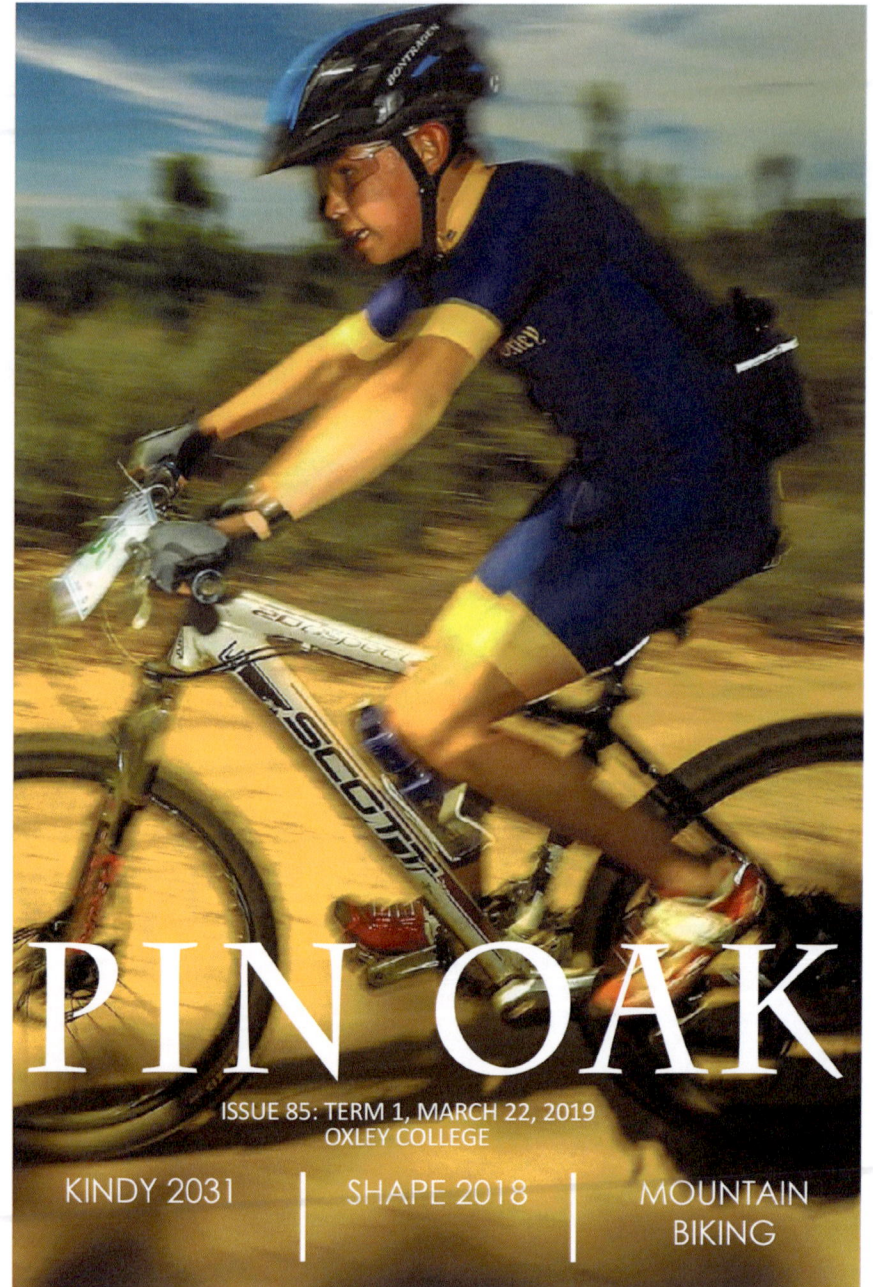

PIN OAK

ISSUE 85: TERM 1, MARCH 22, 2019
OXLEY COLLEGE

KINDY 2031 | SHAPE 2018 | MOUNTAIN BIKING

Students performed at the highest levels in sporting competitions winning trophies in ISA Swimming, Cricket, Hockey, Softball, and Netball. The Junior U11 Football team won the Michael Sant Cup and Aston Satara (Year 8) was selected for the ISA Tennis team. Sophia Dummer (Year 12) was selected for the Open Girls NSWCIS Hockey Team and Emily Bow was selected for the U17 Regional Development Talent Netball Squad. Chilli Sparke (Year 6) was selected for the NSWCIS Primary Hockey Team and named Division 4 Cross Country Freestyle National Champion in Snow Sports. Jamie Gordon (Year 10) travelled to Greece to represent Australia in the U16 Futsal team and the NSW Schools Orienteering Championships were held at Oxley.

The Oxley Equestrian team competed in the 2019 ENSW State Interschool Championships over five days, exhibiting great professionalism, strength, and competitiveness. Anneliese Wansey won the 1.20m Show Jump class, Isabella Price placed second in the overall Medium Dressage Championship and Will David came third in the Advanced Championship. Will also won the Gubbins Pulbrook Group CCN1 Star Junior Division at the Wallaby Hill International Equestrian Event and was selected as Co-Captain of the NSW team for Australian Interschools Equestrian Championships. Anneliese Wansey was selected as Captain of the NSW Combined Equestrian Team.

Head of Junior School Justine Lind resigned to take up a role at Wenona School in Sydney and treasured, long serving staff members, Rob Hughes, Simon Woffendon and Nick Wansey left Oxley after a combined total of more than 45 years.

Above: Equestrian Day with Oxley's Sports Coordinator Nick Wansey and his brother David (left).

Right: Between shows during the 2019 New York Drama study tour. Drama students in Years 10, 11 and 12 attended a dozen Broadway shows, visited Museums and galleries and participated in workshops at leading American Drama Institution, the Stella Adler Acting School

Far right: WOW Day – Wear Orange Wednesday. Students and staff wore orange coloured clothes to show their support and appreciation for State Emergency Services (SES) volunteers. Year 12 student Dylan Whitelaw, an SES volunteer, brought an SES vehicle to school, giving students the opportunity to learn more about the work of the SES.

Below: Parents and Friends Association 'Christmas in July'.

Rituals are a response to impermanence and change - through rituals we express shared beliefs, values and experiences that hold true in spite of change. The tunnel for Year 12s is a ritual - or rite - that marks the passage from one stage of life to another.

Mark Case, Head of Senior School

As Year 12 finished their school year Jenny Ethell said,

This group of Year 12s certainly will hold a special place in my heart and I feel deep gratitude that they have been my first Year 12 cohort ... They are a tight knit inclusive group of young men and women and can be proud of the legacy they will leave for future year groups to follow. Each Year 12 student has made a positive and significant contribution, adding to the fabric of the College through sports, cultural and service activities. They can be very proud of the school spirit they have created.*

This page: Year 12 Farewell tunnel

* *Pin Oak* Issue 95

Opening of Bray Fields on Foundation Day

Above: (left to right) Jenny Ethell, Head Boy Lachlan Moore, Betty Bray, Nicholas Bray, Peter Bray, Head Girl Jemima Taylor and in front, Angus Sheer and Rose Hurst, the youngest boy and girl in the school.

Top right: (left to right) Governors Dennis Mudd, John Rapp, Mandy Lawson, Peter Bray, Betty Bray, Dr Stephen Barnett, Frank Conroy AM, Lachlan Moore, Malcolm Noad, Jemima Taylor, Nicholas Bray, Jenny Ethell, Irene Tritton and in front, Angus Sheer and Rose Hurst.

Bray Fields

The official opening of Bray Fields took place on Foundation Day 2019. Peter Bray was a founding Governor and Treasurer of Oxley College from 1982 to 1989 and Chairman of the Board from 1988 to 1999. In 1981–82 Peter and his wife Betty purchased the property *Riverside Park* in Burradoo, along with 200 acres of adjoining farm land on the southern banks of the Wingecarribee River. In 1985, after discussions with Oxley's founding headmaster, Dr David Wright, the Bray family offered to lease ten acres on the western end of their farm to the College. The formal lease was for 50 years, from 1 January 1986 to 1 January 2036 at $1 per annum rent, with an option to purchase the land at the end of the lease for $100. Instead, in 2019 the Bray Family decided to formally gift the land to the College. Of their decision Peter Bray said:

> Our thinking at the time was to ensure that the land could not be sold off and the funds used for some other school project and to ensure the land could only be used for sporting purposes. Also, if the school did not succeed, it could not be sold off and the funds used to pay creditors. In the same way, the Oxley family lent the school $100,000, which was to be repaid at some stage in the future. Some years later the school had the funds needed to repay the loan, at which time the Oxley family turned the loan into a gift.

> By 2019 the school was fully established and in a very strong financial position. My family agreed that the land was now in safe hands and should be formally gifted to the school and put on its balance sheet as a land asset. The Deed of Gift was formally executed on 18 May 2020, with the title deed in Oxley's name issued on 30 June 2020. The school named the land 'Bray Fields'.

Of the opening of Bray Fields Jenny Ethell said:

> The long awaited playing fields at Bray Fields have been used for the first time this week with our senior rugby and soccer teams playing on the newly established turf. This gift of four hectares (10 acres) of land for sports fields is incredibly generous and will make a considerable difference to the College and our sports program. Having Bray Fields to use as a resource allows the vast majority of our students to train at home and play their home games here on a Saturday.

> As part of our Foundation Day celebrations we held our first tree planting on Bray Fields with trees being planted for the 2019 Year 12 and the Bray family at the entrance. Bray Fields will become our new 'avenue' for the annual Year 12 tree planting. This year we were fortunate to have one of our Board of Governors, former student and parent, Dr Stephen Barnett speak briefly about the advances of the College and how Foundation Day has changed since he was a student. We were also very fortunate to have members of the Bray family and the Board of Governors join all the students and staff for the ceremony.

> Foundation Day is such an important event in the life of the College, recognising the selfless, brave and generous nature of our founders and the incredible journey the College has taken over the past 36 years. It is important to pause and remember the pioneering staff and Oxley families and celebrate the growing maturity of the College and the role it has had in educating thousands of young people. *

Bray Fields have proven to be of immense benefit to the school and as Linda Emery wrote in *A Lovingly Woven Tapestry*, 'The area will remain an enduring legacy of Peter Bray's long commitment to the Oxley College community.'

*Jenny Ethell, Head of College's Report, *Pin Oak* Issue 88, 24 May 2019, p.3

2020

The school year commenced after a summer of devastating bushfires across the Southern Highlands and the east coast of Australia. A few months later the ongoing worldwide coronavirus pandemic changed our lives completely. Social distancing rules were introduced on 21 March and Learning@ home was implemented for all Oxley students. Throughout the year, staff and student leaders developed new and entertaining initiatives to engage the school community during lockdowns, including a variety of creative ISO challenges, such as 'Dress your pet as a Latin Emperor.' Deputy Head of Learning Kathryn Cunich said of this time:

> When I spoke to students and staff at the beginning of the year about our mission 'to equip them for their futures in the exciting, dangerous and uncharted waters of the 21st century', I had been focussed on the bushfires. Little did I know that we would have two back-to-back challenges like the ones we are facing now.

Katherine Halcrow was appointed the new Head of Junior School.

At the start of the year Oxley College partnered with the Applied Positive Psychology Institute to highlight the science of wellbeing and to support Oxley on its Positive Education journey. Fittingly, the theme for 2020 nominated by Oxley's student leaders was Unity: gratitude, teamwork and kindness. The Oxley Student Diary for 2020 integrated PERMAH (Positive Emotion, Engagement, Relationships, Meaning, Accomplishments and Health). It contained information on wellbeing and mindfulness activities, suggestions and opportunities for reflection.

Above: Jenny Ethell with Junior School students
Below: Learning from home

DR STEPHEN BARNETT

Oxley Board of Governors 2012
Chairman 2020 –

Dr Barnett joined the Oxley College Board of Governors in May 2012 and became Chairman of the Board in 2020. He is a Director and a General Practitioner with Highlands General Practice, Managing Director of Medcast, a health professional education company and a Clinical Associate Professor at the University of Wollongong.

Stephen's family moved to the Highlands from Sydney in the late 1980s, after many years visiting the area. After a lovely, long summer holiday in Exeter in 1988 the Barnett family decided they did not want to return to city life. Dr Barnett's mother, a schoolteacher, was keen to relocate and his father, also a doctor, took on a solo GP practice in Bowral.

Stephen and his two sisters are Old Oxleyans. His brother Jeremy and sister Louisa, an Art and STEM teacher in the Junior School until 2023, have children attending the school. Dr Barnett and his wife Catherine, a cellist who teaches cello at Oxley and works with the Oxley Strings Program, have three children,

one is a graduate of Oxley College, while two are current students.

After completing his medical degree at the University of Newcastle, Stephen undertook post-graduate studies in the United Kingdom, gaining a Diploma in Child Health at the John Radcliffe Hospital in Oxford, followed by training as a General Practitioner. He joined Highlands General Practice in 2002.

His research interests focus on the intersection of medical education, health care delivery and information technology. He was awarded a PhD Virtual Communities of Practice in GP training in 2014, is a former Council member of the NSW Royal Australian College of General Practitioners and continues to work, research and teach in medical education. He is also a Graduate of the Australian Institute of Company Directors

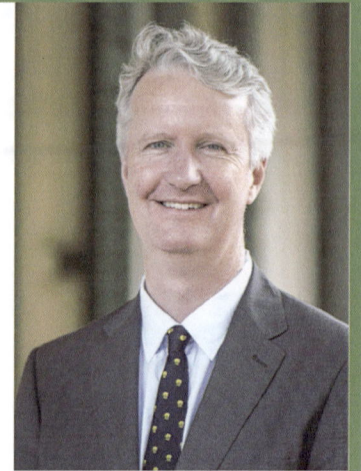

Oxley Governors

Right: (left to right) Malcolm Noad, John Rapp and retiring Chair, Frank Conroy AM

Far right: (left to right) Dennis Mudd OAM, Anni Baillieu and Jan Conroy

The 100th edition of *Pin Oak* was published on 21 February, only weeks before the NSW Government ordered the first lockdown due to risks associated with the escalating global coronavirus pandemic. A bumper issue filled with reflections from former students about their involvement with *Pin Oak*, Head of College report, Jenny Ethell said:

> It is a credit to Mrs Calver and Miss Lanser, who together with the students have brought the original philosophy to fruition of 'not just being a weekly record, rather an exciting interchange of reports, news and views from all parts of the School and beyond.' Student voice is something we value at Oxley and the Pin Oak certainly allows our students to do this in a way which is vibrant and robust, displaying a whole range of interesting perspectives on topics.

The Chairman of the Board of Governors, Frank Conroy AM, retired after 12 years on the Board and Dr Stephen Barnett was appointed as the new Chair. Mr Conroy was the longest serving Chairman in the history of the College and Dr Barnett is the first Oxley graduate to become a governor.

Year 12 students returned to school in May after the first COVID lockdown.

The Oxley Environment Group in conjunction with Landcare Australia resumed work on Wingecarribee River rejuvenation.

School reunions for the classes of 1990, 2000, 2010 took place online via Zoom, as did the Speech Day Assembly at the end of the year.

Issue 100   Term 1, Feb 21, 2020

PIN OAK

OUR 100th ISSUE!

NIC MILNER	BIG ISSUE	ART
The Actual Journey	A Country in Crisis	Murray Walker Prize

Left: Pin Oak *100th Issue cover*
Below: Year 12 Farewell Assembly

More than anything else, 2020 has been a year of expanding our sense of what is possible. In a year when we have been forced to slow down, consume and discard less, we have also witnessed the immediate impact on our environment. The Himalayas have emerged from clouds of pollution and there are patches of blue sky above Beijing for the first time in many years. Fish are returning to clear canals in Venice and, after the rains, rivers are flowing in Australia again. We have even had kaleidoscopic swarms of butterflies on the coast. Will we return to the debate on climate change with a renewed sense of what might be possible?

Just as the fires, floods and pandemic of 2020 triggered a long overdue devaluation of the cult of celebrity and a much needed re-evaluation of what people like the Kardashians have to offer us in a crisis, the year that was has resulted in a greater respect not just for education and a welcome rise in the esteem in which teachers are held, but greater respect for learning more generally and for knowledge. We have all, individually and collectively, had to learn new skills this year, and so perhaps this more intense focus on learning, and its value, is a natural consequence. How many of our students knew what an epidemiologist was before 2020? I am not sure that even I knew precisely. The movement of experts to the forefront of public debate has been both surprising and delightful for someone who values learning in the way that I do. In particular, the increased value that we as a society seem to be placing on science and innovation, listening to the experts rather than popular media, is exhilarating.

For me, in the end, 2020 has been about finding clarity of what stays true. These are our values – kindness, courage and wisdom. These are the things we remain true to when change seems to abound all around us. How do we give those values expression in our community and in our world, and how can we harness that clarity to fight for something better, more meaningful and effective, than the status quo?

The clarity this year has offered us in terms of our individual and collective values, the way in which it has illuminated certain needs and priorities in our world, the challenge it has offered us to develop skills to address these needs as we identify them, all these things are ours to keep.

Extracts from Head of College Jenny Ethell's Speech Day address

With traditional gatherings and marches cancelled, students commemorated Anzac Day from home.

'Cultivate' a new elective for Year 9 was introduced. The focus of the subject is learning to understand key concepts of regional industries.

2020 saw the introduction of new subjects Learning2Learn, Latin, Personal Interest Projects and Personal Ethical Projects, or PIPs and PEPs as they are known. Jenny Ethell said of these initiatives:

> The PIPs and PEPs gifted our students with agency and voice as never before in their learning, and they exercised that agency and raised those voices with great passion and insight. For example, our Year 10 students seized the opportunity to explore topics as diverse as sustainable fabric production and the impact of social media on adolescent mental health, through a variety of methods including metal work, the written word, animation, film making and music. If ever a year taught us that we are limited in education only by the conventional thinking of adults, and traditional notions of schooling 2020 has been it!

Stuart Bollom left Oxley after 17 years of teaching, as did Visual Arts teacher Vanessa Forbes, who retired after more than four decades in education, teaching at various schools. Three of her 2020 Year 12 students had their artwork nominated for ARTEXPRESS, the annual showcase of HSC Visual Arts excellence, with Matthew Hardy's work included in the regional exhibition. During Vanessa's years at Oxley, the works of 23 students were nominated and 11 works were chosen for inclusion in ARTEXPRESS.

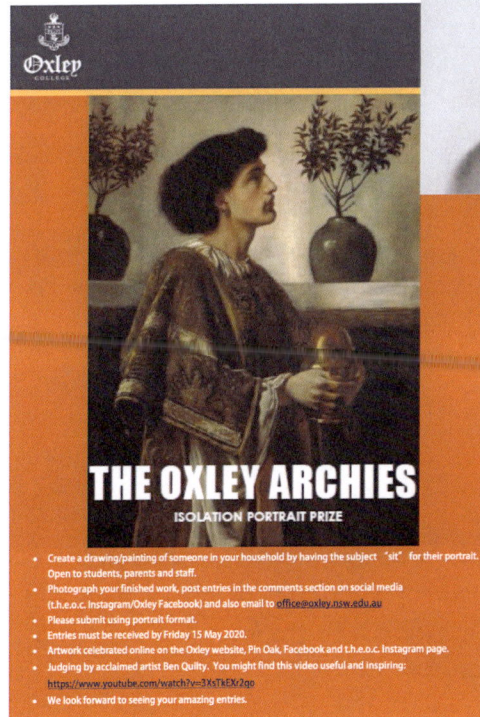

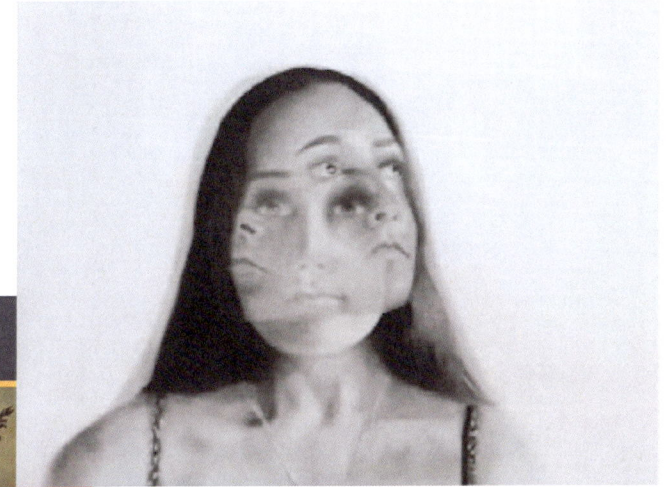

Top: Dimity Deitz work on paper (detail), My Expression of Anxiety

Above: Retiring Visual Arts Coordinator Vanessa Forbes

Left: The Oxley Archies

This page: The 2020 Year 10 Film Festival, held at Oxley due to COVID restrictions

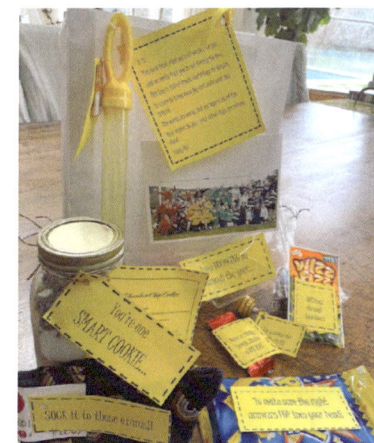

Ava Lambie won the United Nations Voice State Final at NSW Parliament House. Voice is Australia's most prestigious public speaking competition for senior school students, focused on young people's creative solutions to the globe's most pressing issues.

Normal sporting activities were interrupted due to the Coronavirus pandemic. ISA Winter sport recommenced in Term 3 after cancellation due to COVID, however, the competition was affected by further lockdowns in August. At this time Oxley and Chevalier College played against each other in three rounds of local competition. In spite of disruptions there were some notable achievements. Andrew Campbell (Year 7) was awarded a Welsh Cup medal for most improved skier and best sportsmanship at Le Crossett, Switzerland and Chilli Sparke was named Junior Sportsperson of the Year in the Berrima District Sports Award. Annaliese Wansey (Year 12) had multiple wins in Waratah Showjumping events and the Junior A Girls and U14 Boys Basketball teams both won their ISA finals.

Nic Milner (Year 12) won the grueling 25km Australian Alpine Ascent Ultra series in the Snowy Mountains, achieving a personal best time in the process, despite stopping to kindly assist an injured competitor. When asked by Year 12 Academic Master, Molly Simpson, how important running was to his wellbeing, Nic replied:

> It's a struggle for me to not do sport because it is almost like meditation. Actually, I think a lot about my schoolwork when I am running. If I'm struggling with something, I think about it when I run and I usually find a solution.

A full version of Molly's inspiring interview with Nic about his incredible experience can be found in *Pin Oak* Issue 100.

Right: During the height of the COVID lockdown, the Parents and Friends Association delivered 'Cheer up' bags to Year 12 students.
Below: COVID Era performance, filmed for Zoom

Drama productions, *An Inspector Calls*, by J B Priestly, and *Evie and the Birdman*, by John Field were staged.

Rob Parker retired after five years as the inaugural teacher and leader of the Oxley College Pipes and Drums. Barry Gray was appointed to replace him. In a *Pin Oak* tribute Cameron Regan (Year 11) said of Rob,

> ... he leaves a massive impression on those he teaches, not just because of his boundless knowledge of the instrument, but the amazing, engaging stories he shares about his lengthy career in the Piping world. He will be sorely and deeply missed by those he opened the world of Piping to and I wish him well. I must also thank Rob's wife, Mary Lou, for her patience and variety of foods she brings for smoko every Monday. Therefore, I thank both of them for their commitment to not just the band, but the school as a whole.

Year 12 student Aisling Ellis's project 'Gladioli' won the Industrial Design category in the University of Canberra's School of Design and the Built Environment Design Competition.

Charlotte Gray was added to the HSC Honor Roll and ENCORE for her HSC Musicology Viva Voce.

Above right: Pipes and Drums teacher and leader, Rob Parker
Right: Evie and the Birdman rehearsals with Director Phil Cunich
Opposite: Scene from Evie and the Birdman

George was a talented mountain biker. He was known to hit daredevil runs with speed and tenacity, fly through the air performing unimaginable tricks and always had a smile on his face.

Ava Lambie, *Pin Oak* Issue 115

Above: George Dummer at the National Mountain Bike Championships in Victoria, the weekend before COVID lockdown in March.

Left: The GD Champs event

VALE

In 2020 members of the Oxley community were devastated by the deaths of two young Oxleyans, Georgia Kate Beresford (1993–2020) aged 27 years and George Alexander Dummer (2005–2020) who passed away suddenly, aged 14. George's funeral was held at Oxley College on 19 September 2020 during the Coronavirus lockdown. George's older siblings, Charlie (Year 12, 2017) and Sophia (Year 12, 2019) were also students at Oxley.

In George's honour, Oxley's Mountain Bike Coordinator Meaghan Stanton organised the Inaugural Annual GD Champs event. Meaghan said, 'George loved to talk about going to the champs ... the champs this, the champs that, so the event is titled the GD Champs.' Held on 22 November at Welby Mountain Bike Trails, 82 riders participated. Head of College Jenny Ethell said of the day:

> It was a fabulous event and as Meaghan said it was one of the most important and proudest things she has done. The Oxley community turned out in strength to pay tribute to George and the Dummer family. Oxley student, Ava Lambie, wrote a moving article for the local newspaper and as she said, 'there was more than just competition here. People also turned up simply to pay tribute to George, to show support for the Dummer family, to ride with their mates, try their first mountain bike race or just be part of it all.'*

* Head of College's Report, Pin Oak Issue 115, p.3

2020 has been like no other year and on many occasions, we have had to be creative and re-imagine events and traditions. Out of these uncertain times, while there have been some disappointments there has also been unexpected and positive experiences. We have farewelled our Year 12 students this week with all of the traditions that we could hold onto as well as creating some new ones, including having parents at our final Year 12 assembly (livestreamed). The Parents and Friends also enveloped our Year 12s to ensure their finish of schooling was special – the students were both surprised and grateful for the generosity and love shown.

Head of College Jenny Ethell, *Pin Oak*

This page: Year 12 graduation

As a school and as a community, from its inception, Oxley has accepted the inevitability of change and we have been adapting, growing and evolving ever since. Always as pioneers of the future. As the students of Oxley College, from our youngest Kindergarteners to the members of our first ever Year 13, you will become the pioneers of the future, the future of the Southern Highlands, Australia, and the world. It is a future which, just like the past, will be characterised by change.

Extract from Head of College Jenny Ethell's, Speech Day address, delivered via Zoom for the second consecutive year. Year 13 refers to the 2020 Year 12 students who due to COVID restrictions completed some school traditions, like Outback, in 2021

2021

The theme for 2021 was Oxley College: One School. One Focus on Excellence. The COVID-19 global pandemic continued to affect the school community and student life. Ongoing disruptions and lockdowns saw Oxley embrace learning@home. In the Junior School, daily Zoom calls, PowerPoint presentations, 'snapshot' lessons, and the use of online learning platforms like Canvas, Music Lab and Mathletics became the norm, supplemented by 'take home' packs of printed material.

Kathryn Halcrow resigned as Head of Junior School in April and Peter Ayling was appointed Acting Head of Junior School for the remainder of the year. Sue Hanrahan retired after 21 years teaching Science at Oxley. Jenny Ethell thanked Sue, '... for all she has so generously given Oxley – from her teaching, leading of many trips and even knitting neuron and DNA models for Science fairs and exhibitions.' (*Pin Oak* Issue 134)

Oxley Library staff created a click and collect system so that students could continue to borrow books during lockdown. Students could select books though the online catalogue or nominate to receive a surprise.

Planting of 200 native trees and shrubs on College grounds to encourage and support bird life.

Oxley College and the University of South Australia conducted world-first research about learning Mathematics in schools.

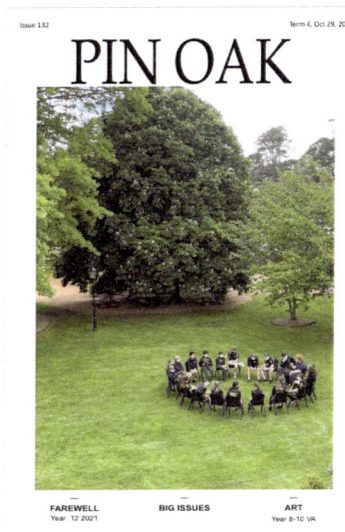

Above: Junior School students.
Opposite: The Year 12 table in The Pavilion.

This page: Learning@home activities included creative challenges, such as these artworks, published in Pin Oak.

Below right: The Librarian's Choice award. Oxley celebrated its second Portrait Prize on Foundation Night 2021. The competition began during 2020 in the depths of COVID-19 as a way to engage the College community in creating art while learning from home. Entries from students, staff and families were judged by Megan Monte and Milena Stojanovska, the Director and Deputy Director of Ngununggula, the Southern Highlands Regional Gallery.

Y7 Art Learning@home

These are some of the ephemeral installations Year 7 created this week around the theme 'circle'.

Their task was to take a walk in nature, even just their backyard, and notice details and collect natural objects to create an artwork.

By Natacha Brochard

VIRTUAL GALLERY

YEAR 10 VISUAL ARTS

Which one is Frida Kahlo's *Self Portrait*, 1940?

Maddy Bragg (Year 10 VAO) has honoured Frida's self-portrait oil painting, with great attention to detail.

She persuaded her model and gathered and incorporated found objects for this photograph.

Meanwhile, Celeste Walker (Year 10 VAX) expertly and delicately places fine porcelain dinnerware for her dog! "Sit" and "Stay"

The original was an oil painting, Barber's *Marco on the Breakfast Table*, 1893

STAGE 2 Art

Stage 2 art were inspired by Canadian Artist Ted Harrison's landscapes.

Kindergarten Art

Kindergarten have been exploring different methods when creating their artworks. This includes using paint, cutting and pushing and drawing their under the sea creations.

YEAR 7 VISUAL ARTS

PORTRAIT

Oxley celebrated its second community Portrait Prize on Foundation Night 2021. We began this competition in the depths of Covid-19 in 2020 as a way to get our community engaged in artmaking while learning from home. This year had many more entries from our students, staff and families. We are so grateful to all who entered and all who viewed this amazing exhibition. A special thank you to Megan Monte and Milena Stojanovska, the Director and Assistant Director of the New Southern Highlands Regional Gallery Ngununggula, which opens later in the year, for judging the prizes.

This year our winners were:

Junior (0-11): Hadley Morgan, Ewan Andrews.

Youth (12-18): Celeste Walker, Lara Fischer, Bronte Joh...

Adults 18+: Lesley Boon, Jodie Swan.

Quilty Award for Excellence and Breaking the Rules: Harris Keith, Annabell Bertollo (Junior).

Family Excellence Award: Hamish Aston (Year 4) and Sue Wilmot (Grandmother), Stella Bacon and Ivy Bacon.

Awards will be presented at our assemblies in Week 7.

THE LIBRARIAN'S CHOICE AWARD

Year 11 Visual Arts

Ava Howes

The David Wright Library at Oxley College comes to life when it houses exhibitions of student artworks. The library space becomes a place that celebrates and acknowledges the efforts and achievements of our student artists. Our students view and discuss the works, enjoying the varied perspectives and techniques used.

To encourage our artists and to thank them for allowing us to display their work, we award a student from each year group exhibition with the "Librarian's Choice" award, a bit like the packing room prize at the Archibald's.

Ava Howes, in Year 11, is the first winner in 2021 for her collection of miniatures. These six small portraits, in vibrant colours, are complex works worthy of stopping to take a closer look. I was impressed by the skilful use of colour, repeated as a theme across each portrait. Although the images are melancholic, the rainbow colours provide hope and a sense of a bright future.

Rory Fenelon (Year 7) won the Wollongong Art Gallery state wide student photography competition, Ava Lambie (Year 12) was named runner up in the Whitlam Institute National Writers Competition and Violet Fitzsimons (Year 8) was a state finalist at the Legacy Public Speaking Competition.

Launch of The Global Thinkers Program (TGS), a vertical ideas discussion forum for students to go beyond their curriculum. Jenny Ethell said the program, '... gives students not just a voice, but the skills and strategies to realise their lofty visions for our world. From micro-credentialling to increasing biodiversity, this is not education for an ATAR, important though it is, this is education for life.'

On 11 November, students and staff gathered for the first time in many months on *Elvo* lawn for the school's annual Remembrance Day Service, commemorating the armistice that brought World War I to an end. With the further easing of COVID restrictions, the postponed House Festival was held over two days, with House groups competing in the areas of drama, art, dance, garage band, Lego and coding (robotics). Announcing the occasion, Head of Senior School Mark Case said, 'Getting as far away from any links with COVID whatsoever, we are looking forward to seeing how creative students will be in interpreting this year's theme of Earth, Wind and Fire.' (*Pin Oak* Issue 133)

An Oxley Cyber Safety Hub was produced by YSafe.

Above: Students and teachers masked up as COVID continues to disrupt school life.

Left: Equestrian Day, Bong Bong.

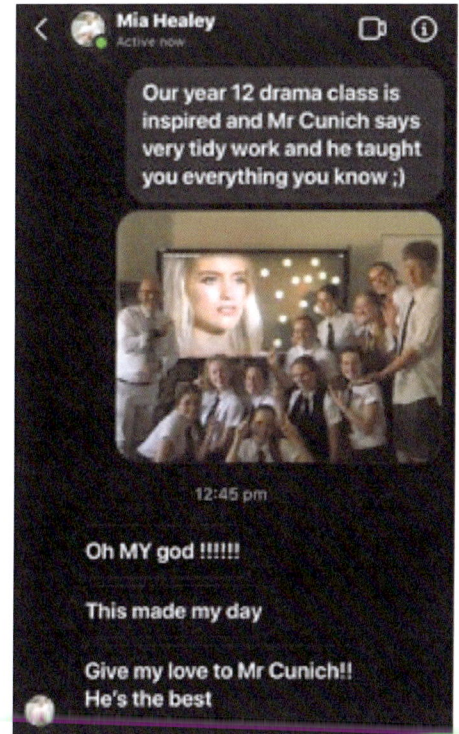

Above: Actor and Old Oxleyan Mia Healey (class of 2016) starred in the Amazon Prime Video series 'The Wilds'. After watching the show's trailer in Drama class, senior Drama students sent Mia a message on social media.

Left and above left: Scenes from Senior School production of Oklahoma.

A Junior Service Learning program saw students visiting or assisting with Harbison Care, Meals on Wheels, Refugees in the Southern Highlands, KIVA (micro finance in third world countries) and Honour our Fallen.

Students Harry Moore, Zane Todorcevski, Joseph Cipolla, Isla Terry, and Ava Gillis competed in the MS (Multiple Sclerosis) 24 Hour Swim and in November Year 12 students, Liv Bow, Molly Knowles, Lily Hogan, Aiofe Barrett-Lennard, Jen Allan and Failie Pulbrook, cut and donated their hair to be made into wigs for people who lose hair due to a medical condition, with funds raised donated to Variety–The Children's Charity.

Oxley College are Dancing for Sick Kids!

Please show your support or join our team and help us make a difference!

Donate here!

Open your phone camera and aim it at the QR code above. You will be directed to a fundraising page where you can make a tax-deductible donation or join our team.

Left: The College community raised $50,000 in the Dance for Sick Kids fundraiser, a 7-day dance challenge in support of Ronald McDonald House Charities and seriously ill children, including Oxley student Emily Hunt and her family.

Far left: Junior School students visiting residents at Harbison Aged Care community.

OUTBACK, MARCH 2021

At the end of Term 1 and into the holidays, a group of Year 12 students embarked on the 33rd Outback trip. The initial journey in 1988 with a small group of Year 11 students was only ever intended to be one trip. Why did it continue? What has motivated teachers and volunteers to drive Toyota Coasters the equivalent of nearly 6 times around the Earth at the equator.

The reasons are so simple: discover your country's beauty and vastness, while learning more about your strengths alongside your peers. But this should not be mistaken as the cliché it may sound. There is also something almost inexplicable about the magic of this journey which many struggle to articulate.

Apart from the expected routines required for covering extensive distances in a timely manner, the only boundaries set for students are with the express intention of 'doing your bit' and care for one another for 15 days. To then share this with teachers and volunteers they know well (not 'experts' or tour guides), this experience becomes unique. It is a simple tradition that carries a spirit passed down through every student who experiences it.

This spirit evolved in the infancy of the trip through the early 1990s. At the core of this spirit: isolation and hardship teaches one about themself; distance and geography connect one to natural beauty and the land in often unexpected ways; the relentless nature of the travel and all its necessities allow one to understand the true meaning of service to one another; and exposure to many varied communities teaches about survival of people and a culture in all its facets.

As staff and volunteers accompanying the 49 students who travelled this year, we returned feeling privileged to have shared this spirit with them all. A generous-of-heart group in every way, they embraced the challenges with humour and grace, and found their own meaning as individuals which will carry them into their last two terms of Year 12. Thank you, Year 12 2021.

Annik Schaefer

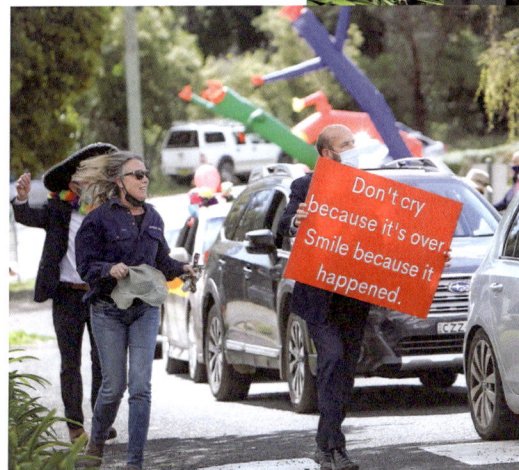

In 2021, Oxley marked the final day for Year 12 students with a vibrant and uplifting 'COVID Safe' drive through celebration followed by a virtual final Year 12 assembly with families in their homes. While very different to the traditional farewell tunnel and formal assembly, students were grateful for this uplifting drive through with music, staff delivering gifts and holding encouraging billboard signs. A memorable example of the agile reimagining of many Oxley events during COVID-19.

JANE CAMPION

Head of the Oxley Junior School 2022 –

Jane Campion commenced as Head of the Oxley Junior School in 2022. Having relocated from Queensland, Jane quickly acclimatised not only to the Highlands weather, but to life at the College. Drawn to the 'magic' of Oxley, she steered the Junior School through its 10th Year and was integral to the Junior School's ongoing growth and success.

Having been Head of a Primary school in Hervey Bay and a Deputy Head of School prior to that, Jane, a passionate educator, was coerced out of the classroom and into leadership because of the depth of knowledge and experience gained from over 30 years in education. 'I am excited to be here in the Southern Highlands and working with such a dedicated team of professionals.'

In 2023, Jane began to re-establish the routines of fulltime schooling for students and staff who were heavily impacted by COVID-19 and the necessities of Home Learning. A warm and engaging leader, she quickly built connections to ensure that the high level of learning and teaching continued through the innovative and progressive programmes on offer in each classroom.

Under Jane's stewardship, the Junior school had much to celebrate in her first year, across both academic and sporting arenas. Highlights included the Year 6 Debating team being awarded first in NSW, another was the Junior School production of Matthew Whittet's, *Fight with all your might the zombies of tonight*. The play presented a key opportunity to celebrate diversity in children while reiterating the importance of inclusivity. 'Each student involved became more confident, resilient and honed their dramatic skills to an exceptional level', shared Jane.

Students enjoyed many excursions and OLE (Other Learning Experiences) Week, where they were able to participate in water and bush activities outside the classroom, from overnight stays on camps in a range of locations, to being actively involved in hands-on problem-solving activities at school. The first edition of 'The Treehouse Papers' was released, full to the brim with articles written by students for students.

Under Jane's guidance the Year 6 leadership program has grown from strength to strength and expanded to include some minor leadership roles in specific areas of interest. Working closely with Year 6 leaders is something that both Jane and Peter Ayling (Deputy Head of the Oxley Junior School) enjoy immensely, giving them the opportunity to listen to students and encourage them to take responsibility for the amazing learning and play spaces they have.

Jane shared, 'We are excited about 'all things Oxley' and celebrate the Junior School as laying the foundational building blocks for our students to be lifelong learners and wonderful citizens of the future.'

2022

COVID safety measures remained in place at the start of the school year. Students were required to test twice a week and send test results through to school.

Jenny Ethell resigned to return to Western Australia during first term and Dr David Mulford was appointed Interim Head of College. Jane Campion commenced as Head of Junior School.

Combined 20 and 30 year school reunions were held at Oxley for the year groups whose reunions were cancelled due to COVID.

Oxley families living in Kangaroo Valley were greatly affected after flooding and landslides caused closure of the road between Fitzroy Falls and Barrengarry Mountain for several months.

In a few of the year's sporting highlights, Phoenix Sparke (Year 10) was selected to compete in the Youth World Biathlon Championships in Utah and sister Chilli Sparke (Year 9) competed in the Austrian Cup as part of the Australian Biathlon Youth Development team. Alister Hill (Year 12) represented Australia in the Men's Individual Epee Junior World Cup in Winterthur, Switzerland in February 2022. Lexie Kennedy (Year 11) was selected to represent the Australian Futsal Association (AFA) 17s Girls team to compete at the 2022 US Futsal National Championship. Annalee Watson (Year 10) was selected for the Cricket NSW Female U16 Country squad and Sam Harwood (Year 8) and Will Torr (Year 9) were selected to play in an International Cricket Academy U17s tournament in India.

Above: Jenny Ethell farewell

Top: Junior School production, Fight with all
Your Might, Zombies of the Night.

Left and above: Scenes from Senior School
production, Antigone.

Groups of Year 11 students from Oxley travel to the Whitsundays, Murrurundi and Katherine Gorge, Mengen, on service-learning trips.

After two years of disruption in the performing arts, the Senior Production of Sophocles' Greek tragedy, *Antigone* was staged. The first performance, however, was cancelled due to severe weather and floods. The Junior School production, *Fight with all Your Might, Zombies of the Night* was performed in June.

Grant Williamson and Justine Lind visited Oxley on Foundation Day, to celebrate the 10th Anniversary of the Junior School.

Oxley Governor Dennis Mudd AO retired after nine years of service to the College.

Two Oxley teams, supported by their Coach and Counsellor, Victoria Rintoul, competed in the final of the annual National Model United Nations Assembly (MUNA) in Canberra. After two days of debating topical world issues against multiple teams of students representing other countries, Oxley's Saudi Arabia team, comprised of Liam Verity, Mackenzie Kane and India O'Brien, won the competition, a significant achievement. India reflected on the experience in *Pin Oak* Issue 146:

> *MUNA was an incredible experience, allowing us students to live out our wildest dreams of saving the world through diplomacy. Adding to the highs of speaking in Old Parliament House and winning the competition, the experience of visiting the Saudi Arabian and Indian High Commissions were also once-in-a-lifetime events.*

This page: The final of the National Model United Nations Assembly (MUNA) at Old Parliament House, Canberra. Liam Verity (above); Liam O'Connell (right); Oxley's combined MUNA team (below).

The Pin Oak that grows magnificently in the heart of Oxley College is a strong symbol of how our young people put their roots deep in the soil and branch out in a unique way, taking their own shape and becoming stronger and more distinct as they grow.

Jenny Ethell, *Pin Oak* Issue 135

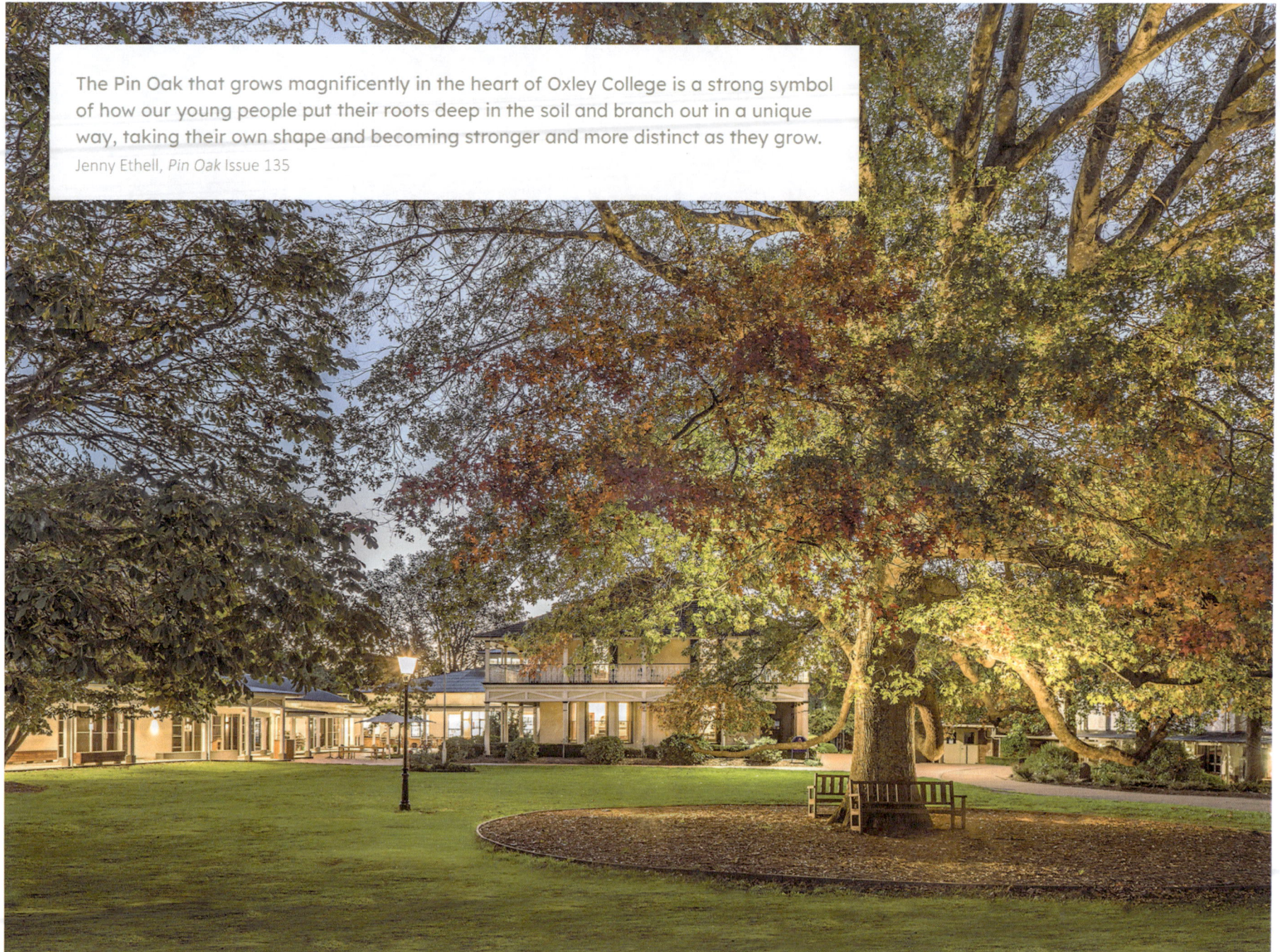

Oxley Junior School's undefeated Year 6 debating team won the New South Wales Debating Final.

The Oxley Pipe Band performed with English singer Robbie Williams during pre-game entertainment at the AFL Grand Final at the Melbourne Cricket Ground.

Student led initiatives during the year included the launching of the Oxley Bee Keeping Club, a 'Unity for Ukraine' fundraising event, and a 'Great Clothes Swap', held by the Oxley Environmental Group.

Year 12 students set off on Outback as their Year 11 trip was cancelled due to COVID. Annik Schaefer joined them on her 20th Outback trip.

Dr David Mulford commenced as Interim Head of College in March 2022 after Jenny Ethell's return to Western Australia. With 27 years experience as a principal, Dr Mulford provided vital stability, wisdom and consistency to the College during the year. His leadership led to significant progress in key areas, including the finalising of the facilities masterplan, the development of the new Strategic Plan to be launched in 2023 and the recruitment of a new Head of College. After leaving Oxley at the end of 2022 and handing over the leadership of the College to Scott Bedingfield, Dr Mulford resumed his much deserved retirement. After a career spanning 48 years, he leaves a substantial legacy. Despite his brief tenure at Oxley, Dr Mulford will be greatly missed for his strength of leadership and vision, as well as his care for everyone in our community and his unfailingly good humour.

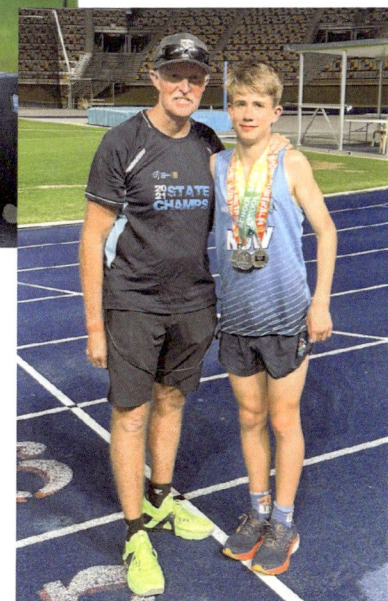

Top right: Dr Mulford and students

Above: Jane Campion at the K–6 swimming carnival

Right: Harry Keats (Year 6) with his coach. Harry competed in the USA Track and Field National Youth Outdoor Championship in New York City and won both the 400m and 800m races. Harry was also named Most Outstanding Athlete in NSW and received the Queen Elizabeth Jubilee trophy for Best Performance Overall at the NSW All Schools State Athletics Championships.

Right and below:
Parents and Friends
Association Trivia
evening

Far right: Support for
Ukraine Day

Violet FitzSimons (Year 9) received the Silver Award in The Queen's Commonwealth Essay Competition.

Year 12 student Ellen Watkin placed equal first in the New South Wales HSC for Earth and Environmental Science.

The 10th Anniversary of the Junior School was celebrated on Foundation Day. Special guests on the day were former Head of College Grant Williamson and former Head of the Junior School Justine Lind, who addressed the school at a Foundation Day assembly.

10th Birthday celebrations for the Junior School on Foundation Day

VALE

Michael Pugh (1958–2022)

The Oxley community were deeply saddened by the death of former Oxley teacher Michael Pugh, who taught at Oxley College for many years, alongside his wife Jacquie Pugh. The father of Old Oxleyans Alex, Oscar and Michaela, Michael was a talented photographer who captured many of the photographs in Oxley's archives. A celebration of Michael's life was held at Oxley on 3 December 2022.

A memorial assembly for Roxanne Spreag was held on 26 August 2022. A Year 11 student in 2003, Roxanne tragically died in a car crash on Norfolk Island during the July school holidays, aged 16 years. Roxy's sister Zanaida Adams attended the special occasion and her friend, Alexandra (Ali) Francipane, an Old Oxleyan and parent, unveiled 'Roxy's Bench' as an enduring memorial. In a moving speech Alexandra said,

> Roxy's bench does not belong to me or my grade, but to the entire Oxley community as a whole. It is everyone's responsibility to remember those we have lost and uphold a special place for them at the College. I really encourage you to use Roxy's bench, not to sit and feel sad about things we cannot change, but to make it a place of fun and laughter where you and your friends can talk, plan, and dream for your futures. My advice – slow down and take joy in the little things, for they surely create the fullest life. In honouring Roxy, please remember – life is short, so live completely and forgive quickly. Love truly, laugh uncontrollably and be sure to make every opportunity count.

Left to right: Tim Dibdin, Zanaida Adams, Alexandra Francipane and Tristan Bevan.

Year 5 and 6 students were invited to include reflections on their year. A few of their responses follow.

In Year 5 I loved the balance between work and fun. With stuff like OLE week and origami to making short movies and learning to play Power Rock, Year 5 was amazing. There was a lot of stuff we did so I can't include it all but some other things are Olympiad, after school clubs, AR and VR and so much more. Year 5 was an amazing year.

– Jameson Clarke, Year 5

In Year 5 I liked all the learning experiences and that every lesson was fun. I liked that if you needed a challenge the teachers would extend you so you could learn more. I like how every lesson you would learn at least one thing. I learnt a lot and had a great time in Year 5.

– Oscar Choo, Year 5

I'm sad my junior school journey is ending but I'm so excited to go and adventure in the Senior School. My past two years here have been wonderful! I've made many friends and overcame many of my challenges. Overall Oxley is an amazing school and has made a big impact in my life.

– Summer Johns, Year 6

The Junior School has been an amazing experience filled with joy; I have made so many lifelong friends that will stick with me forever. I'm looking forward to creating more memories that will be with me throughout my life. I am sad that my time in the Junior School has come to an end, but I look forward to starting my next chapter in life.

– Sophia Dennington, Year 6

Above: Artist and Oxley parent Ben Quilty at the opening of The Studio, Oxley's new Visual Art, Design and Technology building. The Hon Nathaniel Smith MP, along with Directors of local art galleries and parents of Year 11 and 12 Visual Art students also attended.

Left: Head of Junior School Jane Campion addressing Open Day visitors.

2023

Oxley College began a new chapter with the arrival of Oxley's 7th Head of College, Scott Bedingfield and the launch of both the College's 40th Birthday celebrations and the Oxley Foundation. Mr Bedingfield's arrival was marked by a welcome assembly with past and current members of the school community including the Board of Governors, staff, students and parents. Over 350 guests attended the Parents and Friends welcome drinks where there was a real buzz in the Pavilion – at last a return to normality as the community was able to gather again post COVID, fires and floods.

**1983 TO 2023
OXLEY COLLEGE**

SCOTT BEDINGFIELD

Head of College 2023 –

At the beginning of the 2023 school year the Oxley College community welcomed their new Head of College, Scott Bedingfield. 'Having lived in the Camden area for 19 years previously, I had heard of Oxley, and I had been keeping an eye on the school, especially as the vision of Oxley aligns with my own educational philosophy. I am thrilled to have been appointed Head of College and I am very much looking forward to meeting more of our community at Oxley and the wider community of the Southern Highlands,' said Mr Bedingfield.

A former Deputy Principal at St Luke's Grammar School on the Northern Beaches of Sydney, Scott is a career educator. He started out as a Mathematics Teacher and in Outdoor Education, and for 16 years before starting at Oxley, held leadership positions including Outdoor Education Coordinator, Head of Department, Head of Senior School, before taking on the Deputy role.

Commencing his position in Oxley's 40th year signalled not only a new decade, but a new chapter in the history book of Oxley. Mr Bedingfield set the theme for the year as 'regeneration.' (He happily shared that it was borrowed from the senior student leaders of the year.)

'2023 marks a new beginning for our school. We are not going to forget the challenges of the past few years with fires, floods and lockdowns, but we will strive for an improved future for our children. Our senior student leadership team has chosen the idea of 'regeneration' as their focus for 2023 and this is a wonderful way of thinking about what we would like for the year. The idea of bringing back those things which Oxley has been known for but allowing space for new shoots to flourish.'

Scott's family relocated to the Highlands with him, and his daughters attend Oxley. 'Oxley's values of Kindness, Courage and Wisdom are the values I sought for my own children. Oxley is a respectful and inclusive school, working in partnership with our community, valuing academic rigour and experiential education.'

As part of Oxley's new chapter, two significant achievements in 2023 have been the successful launch of the Oxley College Foundation, supporting a Scholarship Fund for students who otherwise would not be able to receive an Oxley education, and the establishment of a Building Fund. Oxley also expanded its program to include Pre-Kindergarten, providing an exciting opportunity for students aged four years to join the College, with a seamless transition to Kindergarten.

Post covid, Oxley returned to its full Distinctives program in 2023 with multiple trips occurring across the College. Our Year 11 students went Outback to Uluru for the first time in many years and Year 10 students travelled to Nepal, rural New South Wales and the Whitsundays. There was also the Year 9 Rites of Passage trip to Canberra and Sydney and OLE week returned to its traditional camps for Years 3 – 8, with an outdoor program offered for K – 2. Oxley's offerings in Outdoor Education and Culture and Service Learning Trips will be expanded over the next few years as we continue to ensure these rich experiences for our students.

Oxley's application to become a Round Square School is its final stages of approval and in October four Year 11 students accompanied Stacey Taylor (Service Learning and Round Square Coordinator) and Scott Bedingfield to Kenya to the World Round Square Conference, meeting students and staff from over 150 different schools across the globe. Further to this we are moving to allowing students in Year 9 the option of having three electives rather than two and an elective will be available for Year 8 students. Students in Year 9 will have 17 total electives to choose from and must include one with an 'international' flavour.

Communications with our community have also been streamlined with a well-received new Oxley App and Parent Portal. Our rich and exciting 40th birthday year, finished with Oxley's whole community Pin Oak Fair in November. There is much to celebrate.

Above: Students showing off their Oxley 40th birthday badges that were given to all students and staff on Foundation Day.

Below and left: Foundation Night celebrating the College's 40th year.

Oxley College Anzac Day Service

Left: Celebrations at the
40th Birthday Ball.

Oxley Athletics carnival

Class KG

Class KL

Class 1S

Class 2D

Class 3B

Class 3R

Class 4A

Class 4W

Class 5K

Class 5N

Class 6H

Class 6S

Year 7

Year 9

Year 11

Year 12

Oxley life

Events and traditions

Oxley College students, staff, parents and carers, the Parents and Friends Association and extended school community have organised and participated in countless events and traditions over the years.

- Foundation Day events and evening, including an address by an Old Oxleyan.
- School performances – theatre and music productions, groups, bands and orchestras.
- Inter-House athletics, cross-country and swimming carnivals.
- Inter-House music, drama, debating and public speaking competitions.
- The awarding of tabs and colours in recognition of excellence in pursuits at College.
- Year 7 History Archeological dig at the Minnows.
- Year 7/8 Medieval Feast for history students (commenced 2004) and local Aboriginal study excursions.
- Oxley Playwriting Festival (commenced 2008)
- Year 12 HSC Visual Arts, Design and Technology exhibitions and Drama showcase.
- Music Night, featuring the college ensembles and Year 12 HSC music performances.
- Year 10 School Certificate (held until 2011).
- Mock Trial competition, conducted by the Law Society of New South Wales.
- MUNA – Model United Nations Assembly. Oxley's participation is sponsored by the Bowral-Mittagong branch of Rotary International.

PIN OAK

CROSS COUNTRY | CHICAGO | WELCOME MR BEDINGFIELD

- Various inter-school, national and international mathematics, science, geography, history and engineering competitions and challenges, including GATEway8, the International Competition and Assessment for Schools (ICAS), NSW Premier's reading challenge and Tournament of Minds NSW.

- Music festival camp and concert hosted by Heads of Independent Co-educational Schools (HICES).

- National Youth Science Forum (NYSF).

- Parent and carer/student/teacher meetings and information sessions.

- Careers expo for senior students.

- Speech Night, the final event of the school year, where academic, sport and annual awards are presented.

- Year 7 orientation camp at the start of the year. A wonderful opportunity for new students to get to know each other and their Year 12 House leaders.

- Sporting events – including athletics, tennis, fencing, snow sports, softball, basketball, cricket, football, tennis, swimming, netball, rugby, hockey, cross country, kayaking, mountain biking, equestrian and water polo.

- Senior and Junior Equestrian Day, held for many years at Araluen, the property of generous hosts the late Dr John Roche and Mrs Kathy Roche.

- Outdoor Learning Experience (OLE) adventures for Years 3–10. Experiences have ranged from visiting the mosques of Istanbul to cross country skiing, scuba diving, surfing, or assisting the homeless.

- Overseas service opportunities (OSSO) Year 9–10 support for communities in Botswana, Fiji and Nepal.

- Visits from English language exchange students, including annual visits between 2005 and 2018 from the Dutch school KSG Apeldoorn (Koninklijke Scholengemeenschap).

- Year 11 leadership camp where students plan ideas, goals and aims for Year 12 life.

- Inter-School competitions – public speaking, debating, the Shakespeare Festival and sports carnivals, including Chevalier Shield Athletics, HICES and ISA carnivals.

- Junior School Book Week parade and Grandparent Day.

There are traditions and cultures aplenty at Oxley. Some have been in place since inception, others only quite new. All of them collectively help weave the unique experience that is a childhood spent within the protection of Oxley College. *Michael Parker, 2016*

- Fast and Fresh Short Play Festival (since 2007). Plays must be under 10 minutes in length and devised, written, performed and directed by students 18 years or younger.
- Year 12 formal and farewell events, including a breakfast, informal assembly and formal assembly, whole school farewell tunnel and dinner.
- Year 10 Australian Business Week (ABW) a five-day program during which students participate in competitive business simulations. Teams are required to run their own simulated company, develop a product idea and a set of promotional strategies designed to appeal to a new market. The week concludes with a presentation dinner.
- Year 9 Rites of Passage. An 'Oxley Distinctive' that commenced in 2016, students spend two weeks (originally three weeks) in Sydney undertaking a variety of activities designed to expose them to ideas, people and phenomena outside the classroom.
- End of year talent quest on the last day of the school year. A popular event and a lot of fun, on many occasions the final item was a song played by the staff band.
- Parents and Friends Association functions, both formal and social, including trivia evenings, equestrian day and gymkhanas, textbook exchange, golf tournaments, balls, dances, picnics, fairs and festivals.
- Back to Oxley Day for Old Oxleyans (introduced 2007) and Oxleyan class reunions, held every 10 years.
- Cricket match between Old Oxleyans and the Firsts XI Cricket team.
- Mission Day, organised by the Student Representative Council (SRC) featuring an array of exciting activities and food to raise money for various charities. The final event is the Inter-House tug-of-war competition. The SRC also organise school discos.
- Participation in the Bowral Anzac Day march through Bowral and the Remembrance Ceremony at Bowral War Memorial Park.
- College open and orientation days.
- Christmas carol service.

- The Festival of Ideas.
- **Duke of Edinburgh's International Award** – a voluntary program that has been enriching the lives of young people in over 140 countries since 1956. First introduced at Oxley in 1992, participants design their own unique program of challenges and goals, developing strength, resolve and commitment. Open to young people aged 14 to 25, the program is available at Bronze, Silver and Gold levels. To achieve the prestigious Gold Award, students complete at least 105 hours of community service, six adventurous journeys across the State, totalling at least 18 days in a wilderness setting; two years commitment to developing personal interests and practical skills; physical recreation of 90 hours, and a five-day residential program. In 2008, 15 Oxley students received their Gold Awards at Government House, where Her Excellency, the Governor General of New South Wales, Marie Bashir, described Oxley's program as one of the best in the country. In 2016, during the Diamond Jubilee celebrations of the DOE in Australia, attended by Prince Edward the Duke of Wessex, Oxley received a special recognition award presented by Margaret Beazley at Government House. In 2022, nine Oxley students received their Gold Award and as of May 2023 there are about 180 students actively participating in the program. Oxley's DOE Award Leader, Tim Dibdin, has led the popular program for many years, assisted by Jenni Rees.
- **Outback** – A Year 11 learning adventure designed to challenge, inspire and unite the year group before their final school year. Devised by Helmut Schaefer in 1988, the 14 or 15 day experience to the centre of Australia is a much loved rite-of-passage and the pinnacle of Oxley's OLE experience. Below, a reflection from a student:

This ... our majestic and awe-inspiring country,
where the land stretches to meet the domed sky
in a burning copper shimmer,
where sunspears turn the air
to molten glass.

House System and Mentor Groups

The House and Mentor Group system at Oxley fosters loyalty, commitment and a sense of belonging. It encourages friendships and bonds of mutual care to develop between junior and senior students and aims to ensure every student is known and supported throughout their school life by at least two adults, their Head of House and their Mentor.

Oxley's House activities emphasise participation rather than competition. Houses are named after significant pioneers in various fields of endeavour. They reflect qualities that Oxley aims to develop in students – a sense of challenge, acceptance of responsibility, spiritedness, sensitivity, compassion and awareness of the needs of others.

An article regarding the origins of the House names, published in the 1983 Oxleyan magazine states:

> From the start, the house system was introduced at Oxley, the two Houses being temporarily named North and South. In the meantime, the search for permanent House names was instigated. It was felt that since the College has taken its name from John Oxley (and his links to the district) that the explorer theme should be followed, although the word exploration was given its widest possible interpretation and Australian explorers of science, art and literature were considered as well as those who opened up new geographical territories. It soon became apparent that there were numerous candidates for our task, and that the name search could drag on indefinitely. However, a list was finally compiled and eventually four names were selected, representing exploration in its widest context. Those selected were Douglas Mawson (Antarctic explorer/geologist), Howard Florey, (scientist), William Dobell (artist) and John Monash (military genius/engineer). Mawson (North) and Florey (South) were immediately adopted in 1983 and the two additional Houses, Dobell and Monash will come into existence in 1984.

More about the Australian pioneers after whom Oxley's Houses are named can be found on pages 179–185 of *A Lovingly Woven Tapestry, Oxley College Bowral 1983–2004.*

In Years 7–12 students are allocated to one of six Houses. Each House is then divided vertically into Mentor Groups of approximately 15 students, with each year group represented, all under the guidance of a member of staff – their Mentor. Mentor groups meet every school day, with full Houses coming together regularly

We have such energy in our House that it can barely be contained, often spilling out in the loveliest of ways as people simply enjoy each other's company and all the varied experiences that come with the House system at Oxley.

Jo McVean, Head of Durack (Oxleyan 2008)

House	Category	Role	Name
Dobell Culture		Artist	**Sir William Dobell** (1899–1970)
Durack Sport		Olympic swimmer	**Sarah Durack** (1899–1956)
Florey Research		Scientist	**Lord Howard Florey** (1898–1968)
Mawson Exploration		Explorer	**Sir Douglas Mawson** (1898–1958)
Monash Public Service		Leader	**Sir John Monash** (1865–1958)
Oodgeroo Literature		Poet and civil rights leader	**Oodgeroo Noonuccal** (1920–1993) formerly known as Kath Walker

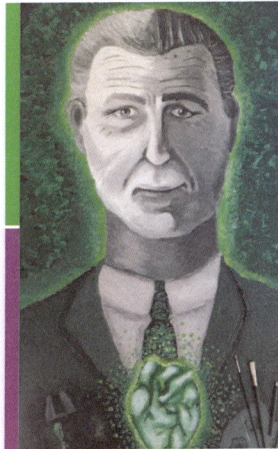

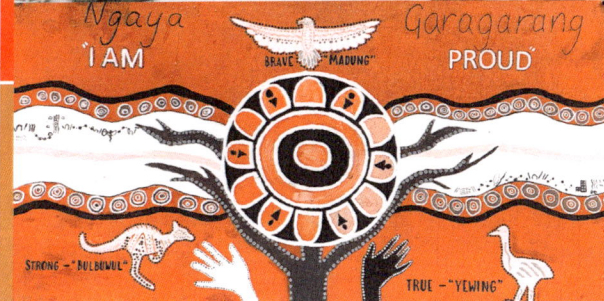

Continuing the Oxley theme, the Junior School Houses are named after Australian pioneers in various fields.

Chisholm
Kindness

Social activist and philanthropist
Caroline Chisholm
(1880–1951)

Flynn
Wisdom

Founder of the Royal Flying Doctor Service
Reverend John Flynn
(1880–1951)

Walton
Courage

Pioneering aviatrix. Became known as the Angel of the Outback
Nancy Bird Walton
(1915–2009)

On their last day of school some of the 2016 Year 12 students dressed up as their house inspirers. Clockwise from top left: Brandon Colby (Dobell), Kaarina Allen (Durack), Ben Quirico (Mawson), Cate Patterson (Chisholm), Emma Croker (Walton), Alex Cox (Monash), Christopher Alexov (Florey).

A day in the life of Oxley College 2023

'It takes a village to raise a child', so the African proverb goes. What then does it take to run a school? At Oxley it takes a large community of dedicated, passionate professionals, volunteers, parents and carers, a diverse team working collectively at a multitude of different tasks, for a cohort of more than 800 students, who are the reason Oxley College exists.

On any given school day during school term, dozens of staff and volunteers can be found at Oxley. Like musicians in an orchestra performing a symphony, bees buzzing around their hive, or the billions of individual cells that combine to create the incredible human beings we all are, everyone in the Oxley community has a role to play. We all know our own part, but how well do we understand what some of the other roles entail?

The table (right) shows a few of the many activities that might occur during an Oxley day.

6.00 (am)	Maintenance team arrive. Cleaners check and clean the bathrooms – there are 59 toilets across the school!
7.00	Some students attend sport training, music practice or extra-curricular activities.
7.30	Most administration staff arrive between 7am and 8am.
8.00	Academic and other support staff start their day. College visitors sign in at reception upon their arrival and departure. Dozens of scheduled visitors are welcomed to Oxley during any week.
8.30	Library opens and canteen volunteers and assistant staff start. The clothing pool opens at least three days a week
8.40	Transition bell, House mentor groups meet
8.45	Period 1
9.40	Period 2
10.30	Recess
10.55	Recess ends
11.00	Period 3
11.50	Period 4
12.40	Lunch – Groups sometimes meet during lunch break. The *Pin Oak* Team meet on Mondays, to discuss content for the coming issue
1.20	Lunch ends
1.25	House Mentor Groups meet
1.45	Period 5
2.40	Period 6
3.25	Classroom lessons conclude. Sports training takes place on at least two afternoons after school. Co-curricular clubs, such as the Art or Study Club meet
4.00	Academic staff officially finish at 4pm, but they are often at school until much later, particularly if they have after school events, co-curricular or sporting duties and activities. Cleaners commence their work
5.00	Various meetings may take place after school and during the evenings
6.00	Library closes
7.00	Regular visitors to The Pavilion – magpies, currawongs and other animals, including neighbourhood dogs and the odd blue tongue lizard are encouraged to leave by the cleaners
8.00	Cleaning team finish
9.00 (pm)	After evening events at the school conclude, the resident nocturnal wildlife rule the roost until dawn. Many possums, birds, cats and their families have called Oxley home over the years

Oxley College Sport

Enthusiasm, participation, teamwork, commitment, persistence, resilience, humility, a willingness to learn and improve and wonderful sportsmanship are just a few of the attributes that characterise sporting life at Oxley.

Sport has always been an important and integral part of education at Oxley. To feature the multitude of individual and team sporting highlights and successes achieved over the years would require a book of its own, perhaps even a book for each sport. More importantly, in the end it's not winning that matters, it's how the game is played. Memorable moments included throughout these pages are representative of the variety of athletic pursuits and skills developed and enjoyed by our students.

During the school term training and lessons take place from 7am until 7pm. Early Saturday morning set offs and long bus trips to host schools on the Central Coast, Sydney or beyond are considered all part of the fun for our sporting teams. Oxley athletes are ably supported by dedicated coaches and teachers who share their knowledge, skills, time and energy and by parents who act as mentors, taxi drivers, first aid officers, catering staff and sideline supporters.

Oxleyans have been involved in many sporting pursuits over the years, achieving outstanding personal and team results in local, state, national and international sporting arenas. Groups of Oxley athletes have toured across the country and around the world to play or compete and Oxley has proudly hosted countless visiting sporting teams.

Oxley students have participated in:

Athletics	Gymnastics	Softball
Basketball	Hockey	Swimming
Cricket	Kayaking	Tennis
Cross Country	Mountain Biking	Touch Football
Equestrian	Netball	Water Polo
Fencing	Rugby	
Football	Snowsports	

Hockey reflects life.
Always strive to do
your best. Never give
up. Especially when
the going is tough and
develop tolerance,
commitment, and respect
for others.

Barbara Alexander
(Oxleyan 2008)

Oxley College School Song

The College has adapted 'Fill the World with Love' as its school song. Written by Leslie Bricusse for the Metro-Goldwyn-Mayer production of 'Goodbye Mr Chips', the words are regarded as not only applicable to the life of that redoubtable schoolmaster, but also to the growth of the College and to all members of the Oxley family.

In the morning of my life
I shall look to the sunrise,

At a moment in my life when the world is new.

And the blessing I shall ask is that God will grant me,

To be brave and strong and true.

And to fill the world with love my whole life through.

And to fill the world with love,

And to fill the world with love,

And to fill the world with love my whole life through.

In the noon time of my life
I shall look to the sunshine,

At a moment in my life when the sky is blue.

And the blessing I shall ask will remain unchanging,

To be brave and strong and true.

And to fill the world with love my whole life through.

And to fill the world with love,

And to fill the world with love,

And to fill the world with love my whole life through.

In the evening of my life
I shall look to the sunset,

At a moment in my life when the night is due.

And the question I shall ask only you can answer,

Was I brave and strong and true?

Did I fill the world with love my whole life through?

Did I fill the world with love?

Did I feel the world with love?

Did I fill the world with love my whole life through?

Oxley College School Hymn

The music for the College Hymn has been adapted from Ludwig von Beethoven's Ninth Symphony, the last movement, often called 'Ode to Joy'. This beautiful movement was the last of Beethoven's symphonies, and it is believed to have been written when the musician had come to terms with the deafness from which he was suffering.

The words of the hymn were written by the founding Oxley Headmaster, David Wright.

Let us join in earnest striving, for the good of Oxley's name.

May it rise to heights of greatness, right to glorious honour claim;

Humble in the search of knowledge, careful in the use of word,

Firmly holding faith and goodness, loyal to our land, our Lord.

May it take to life the measure, proving the eternally true,

Dauntless in the face of challenge, keeping the high goal in view,

Striding in the pioneer's footprints, risking the unknown terrain,

Patience may it be our escort, constant fortitude our aim.

Appendix

Oxley Board of Governors

Baillieu, Anni	2016–present*	
Barnett, Dr Stephen	2012–present*	Chairman 2022– present
Barsby, Donald R	1983–1984	
Berkelouw, Leo I	1982–1990	
Bray, Peter M	1982–1999	Chairman 1988–1999
Calver, Emma M	2003–2006	
Campbell, Robert B	1999–2002	
Carpenter, William McI	1982–1996	
Chambers, Margaret A J (OAM)	1982–1986	
Conroy, Frank (AM)	2008–2020	Chairman 2009–2020
Crowley, Jane	2021–present*	
Duckmanton, Lady Janet	1997†	
Duncan, Heidi	2006–2007	
Edwards, Jan	2005–2006	
Emery, Linda	2006–2017	
Farrow, Professor Brian R H	2003–2011	
Fitzpatrick, Marie H H	2001–2009	
Freire, Kristina S	2002–2006	
Hanrahan, Brian H	1999–2005	Chairman 1999–2005
Harrison, Stephen B M	1982–1992	
Hoskins, Donald G	1982–1988	Founding Chairman 1982–1988
Hoskins, Rosemary A	1990–1997	
James, Geoffrey R	1991–1999	
Joubert, Eugene	2008–2015	
Keith, Kirsten	2021–present*	
Kirsch, Brian	2022–present*	
Lawson, Mandy	2012–2023	
Lemann, F Martin	1997–2009	
Mackay, Hugh	2015–2016	Special adviser to the Board
McAllery, Roderick	2017–present*	
McKenzie, Dr Ian C	1982–1989	
Macmaster, D John F	1987–1990	
Macmaster, Judith A	2000–2001	
Melrose-Rae, Douglas	2023–2023††	
Mudd, Dennis (OAM)	2014–2022	
Naughton, Julie	2007–2016	
Nicholas, M Jane	1987–1999	
Noad, Malcolm	2017–present*	
Norrie, Tony	2009–2021	
Osborne, James A	1998–2001	
Pritchard, Dr John R	1994–2005	
Rapp, John	2014–2023	
Roche, Dr Vincent J	2001–2012	
Rowe, Richard	2005–2012	
Sanderson, Andrew	2023–present*	
Smee, Dr Grahame M	1982–1999	
Tendys, Richard	1982–1986	
Walker, Murray M (OAM)	2001–2012	Chairman 2005–2009
Walton, Jane	2006–2008	
Webber, Erica A	1992–2001	
Wheeler, Phyllis M	1998–2001	
White, Dr Ronald E	1986–1993	
Windeyer, Christine	2016–present*	

*As of October 2023

†Lady Duckmanton was appointed to the board in 1997 but a subsequent appointment prevented her from taking up the position.

††Douglas took up a position on the Board of AISNSW which required him to resign from Oxley's Board.

Parents and Friends Association **Presidents**

1983	Bill Watson
1984 – 1985	John Colless
1986 – 1987	John MacMaster
1988 – 1989	Robert Jones
1990 – 1991	Robin Mogg
1992 – 1993	John Pritchard
1994 – 1995	Susan McGowan
1996	Tony Bennett
1997	Stephen Brown
1998	Richard Connor
1999	Rob Riddel
2000	Susan Ingram
2001	Warren Reece
2002	Bob Pigott
2003	Helen Jones
2004	Rob McCarthy
200?	John Wasiliev
2007	Phil Chapman
2011	Denis Thomas
2012	Tina Allen
2014	Cindy Pryma
2016	Trevor and Kate Fair (caretakers)
2017	Bec Biddle
2020 – 2023	Megan Moore

Foundation Day **Guest Speakers**

There were no guest speakers at Foundation Day Ceremonies, from 1983 until 1997, when it was decided to invite past students from 10 years ago, to speak.

1996	Dr David Wright – opening of the David Wright Library
1997	Dr Jane Gray (nee Schwarz)
1998	No guest speaker
1999	Matthew Smee in honour of founding Governor, Dr Grahame Smee, who died earlier in the year, and Troy Myers
2000	Annik Schaefer
2001	Dr David Duke
2002	Suzanne Novak (nee Kite)
2003	Sam Jones
2004	Ainslie Ashton
2005	Sassica Myers
2007	Dr David Wright and Fergus Hanson
2009	Louisa Barnett Royds
2010	Alex Kanaar
2011	Ruqayya Ahmed
2012	Sacha Mielczarek
2013	Jess Roche
2014	Henry Bradley
2015	Charlotte Hanson
2016	Andrew Rumsey
2017	Alicia Wells
2018	Matt Perger
2019	Annabel Blake
2020	No Old Oxleyan due to COVID
2021	Belinda McNaught
2022	Sam Jones
2023	Jane Macmaster

Heads of School

1982–1993	Dr David HM Wright	
1994 (January) – 1994 (August)	Anthony J Nutt	
1994 (September) – 1995 (June)	Peter T Craig	(Acting)
1995 (July) – 2007	Christopher J Welsh	
2008 – 2014	Grant Williamson	
2014 – 2018	Michael Parker	
2019 – 2022 (March)	Jenny Ethell	
2022 (March – December)	Dr David Mulford	(Interim)
2023 – present*	Scott Bedingfield	

Head of K–6 Department

2012 – 2013	Steven Armstrong

Heads of Junior School

2015 – 2019	Justine Lind	
2020 – 2021 (April)	Kathryn Halcrow	
2021	Peter Ayling	(Acting)
2022 – present*	Jane Campion	

*As of October 2023

Head Boy and Head Girl

1987	Mark Lowe and Jane Schwarz
1988	Andrew Fennell and Patricia Varvel
1989	Troy Myers and Jenny Wood
1990	James Landrigan and Annik Schaefer
1991	Joshua Englebrecht and Kathryn Gray
1992	Grant Hackelton and Joanna Sommerville
1993	Glen Tommy and Sarah Bladen
1994	Simon Fergusson and Ainslie Ashton
1995	Christopher Khan and Madeleine Challander
1996	Christopher White and Katherine Nevett
1997	Reece Turner and Amber Phelps
1998	Andrew Eastaway and Susan Cochrane
1999	James Tonkin and Lara Craig
2000	William Gell and Brooke Allen
2001	Joel Hodder and Alessandra Ryde
2002	Sasha Mielczarek and Camille Williams
2003	Tobias Hanson and Kate Jeuniewic
2004	John Philipson and Alison Connor
2005	Trevor Delbridge and Charlotte Hanson
2006	Andrew Rumsey and Camilla Bradley
2007	Timothy Kime and Karen McGrath
2008	Edward Bradley and Eleanor Keft
2009	Nathaniel Willoughby Katrina Allman
2010	Winston Bradley and Montana Mays
2011	William Lawson and Charlotte Blake
2012	Phillip Syrros and Sophie Krieger
2013	Daniel Bollom and Eleanor Naughton
2014	Luther Canute and Zoe Binder
2015	Zac Moran and Evangeline Larsen
2016	Brandon Colby and Cate Patterson
2017	Thomas Hill and Isabella Knowles
2018	Harrison Baillieu and Olivia Donovan
2019	Lachlan Moore and Jemima Taylor
2020	Connor Taylor-Helme and Clancy Aboud
2021	James Feetham and Mia Gillis
2022	Hal Canute and Peggy Holmwood

School Captains

2023	John Smedley and Leah Halstead

Junior School Captains

2012	Olivia Davies and Oscar Moran
2013	Andrew Bailey-Hughes and Tully Mahr
2014	Alicia Brain and Luke Pierobon
2015	Medeleine Sargeant and James Feetham
2016	Brianna Grice and Jack Hatcher
2017	Sophie Dunn and Billy Cameron
2018	Sophia Hamblin and William Barnett
2019	Arkie Francis and Harley Evans
2020	Flynn O'Brien and Imogen Gair
2021	Aiden D'Iorio and Matilda Lambie
2022	Louis Robertson and Grace Kean
2023	Theodore Blom and Pixie Hanson

Grahame Smee Scholarship

2000	Cornelia Alchin
2001	Georgia Stannard
2002	Kate Jeuniewic
2003	Poppy Dowsett
2004	Dominic Mercer

Oxley Award

Presented on Speech Night, the Oxley Award is the premier Award of the College. It is awarded to a Year 12 student who in the judgement of the Awards Committee, has in all four fields: academic, cultural, leadership and sport, achieved the best overall performance. Levels of service to the College and community are also taken into account when selecting the recipient. The name of the recipient is inscribed on the Honours Board of the College.

Note: Unlike the Head Prefect and Dux, the Oxley Award did not start until 1988. The list in *A Lovingly Woven Tapestry*, started at 1987, however, the Honours Board started in 1988.

1988	Joanna Nicholas	2008	Eleanor Keft
1989	Jenny Wood	2009	Katrina Allman
1990	James Landrigan	2010	Montana Mays
1991	Joshua Englebrecht	2011	Stephanie Allman
1992	Grant Hackleton	2012	Gabrielle Nappa
1993	Melissa Gray	2013	Michael Turczynski
1994	Emma Sydenham	2014	Zoe Binder
1995	Sassica Myers	2015	Zac Moran
1996	Prue Alexander	2016	Heidi Bevan
1997	Reece Turner	2017	Rosemary Bowyer
1998	Andrew Eastaway	2018	Benjamin Hutchings
1999	Hannah Raffe	2019	Jade Gillis
2000	Claire Ingram	2020	Joshua Bramley
2001	Joanna Khoo	2021	Ava Lambie
2002	Camille Williams	2022	Hal Canute
2003	Tobias Hanson	2023	Sophie Dunn
2004	Alison Connor		
2005	Andrew Harris		
2006	Katherine Delbridge		
2007	Taryn Harris		

DUX

1987	Robert Stuart	2014	Laura Farag
1988	Guy Lampert	2015	Evangeline Larsen and Grace Naughton
1989	Jane MacMaster		
1990	Timothy Mallam	2016	Jaime Pryor
1991	David Duke	2017	Lillian Dalton
1992	Marcus Stowar	2018	Kathryn Dalton
1993	Gerlinde Gniewosz	2019	Skye Holmwood
1994	Vanessa MacFarlane	2020	Maxwell Lambie and Claire Allan
1995	Sassica Myers		
1996	Kylie Quinlivan and Christopher White	2021	Ava Lambie
		2022	Mackenzie Kane
1997	Christine Gee	2023	Leah Halstead
1998	Liam Burgess		
1999	Peta Khan		
2000	Benjamin White		
2001	Erin Cartledge		
2002	Lisa Connor		
2003	Ingrid Parker		
2004	Gemma Dawkins		
2005	Emma Mainprize		
2006	Jessica Byrnes		
2007	Amy Davis		
2008	Albert Woffenden		
2009	John Downes		
2010	Lara Miller		
2011	Morgan Sheargold		
2012	Paul Dempster		
2013	Eleanor Naughton and Michael Joubert		

Acknowledgements

Communities are wrapped in human memory. During the many hours I spent exploring Oxley's extensive archives in the attic above the Design and Technology classrooms, I was frequently amazed. Amazed by the activities, abilities, accomplishments and joy captured in thousands of photos and documents amassed over the past 40 years. Amazed also – flabbergasted really – at the vision, determination, incredible hard work and persistence of the many dedicated men and women who dared to dream and committed their considerable skills, energy, experience, time and money into creating an independent, co-educational school in the Southern Highlands. Without them Oxley College simply would not exist. Many of these people – Oxley's pioneers – did not even have children at the school.

Thanks to them and to those who have followed, Oxley College has a lot to remember and reflect upon. History nurtures identity in a world characterised by difference and change. It supports a sense of community and place. The years fly by, memories fade and we become caught up in the busyness of the now. The school is so lucky to have its first 21 years recorded in Linda Emery's book, *A Lovingly Woven Tapestry, Oxley College Bowral 1983–2004*. Thankfully, Jenny Ethell and Emma Calver recognised the importance of recording and sharing some of the College's life since then. Together, both these books are a valuable record of the community that is Oxley College.

Jenny and Emma, my heartfelt thanks go to you for your vision, passion, help and support. Thank you Linda Emery, for your inspiration, encouragement and for establishing the Oxley archives, along with Joanne Richards, Trish Topp, Ros Hamilton and others. Many Oxley records would already be lost without your efforts to collect and preserve them.

Thank you to all the talented and dedicated teachers and staff at Oxley – I am in awe of your passion and energy for what is a very consuming profession. Thank you for answering all my questions and emails and providing wonderful material for the book.

Thank you to Megan Moore and Amberley Guilly for your support and help with photographs and year reviews, and to Natalie Lane for proofreading the book. Sincere thanks also to Em Cassin, Peter Bray, Michael Parker, Dr Stephen Barnett, Frank Conroy, Christopher Welsh, Grant Williamson, Peter Craig, Annik Schaeffer, Jason and Molly Simpson, Kate and Phil Cunich, Tim Dibdin, Tristan Bevan, Linda Rees, Joy Burgess, Fiona Nixon, Alex Stone and Alina Fischer.

Natalie Bowra, thank you for your beautiful book design and for holding my hand through the whole process. Working with you and Emma Calver has been a true pleasure.

Finally, to my husband Ashley, thank you for your loving support and for providing some of the beautiful images in the book, and to my own Oxleyans, Max (Class of 2017) and Eva (2019) thank you for giving me the opportunity to be an Oxley Mum.

Amanda Mackevicius
Author

For your digital copy of *A Lovingly Woven Tapestry, Oxley College, Bowral 1983–2004* please scan the QR code or visit the Oxley College website About Page
www.oxley.nsw.edu.au/about/the-college

RECOLLECTIONS

RECOLLECTIONS

www.ingramcontent.com/pod-product-compliance
Lightning Source LLC
Chambersburg PA
CBRC101827090426
42811CB00023B/1920